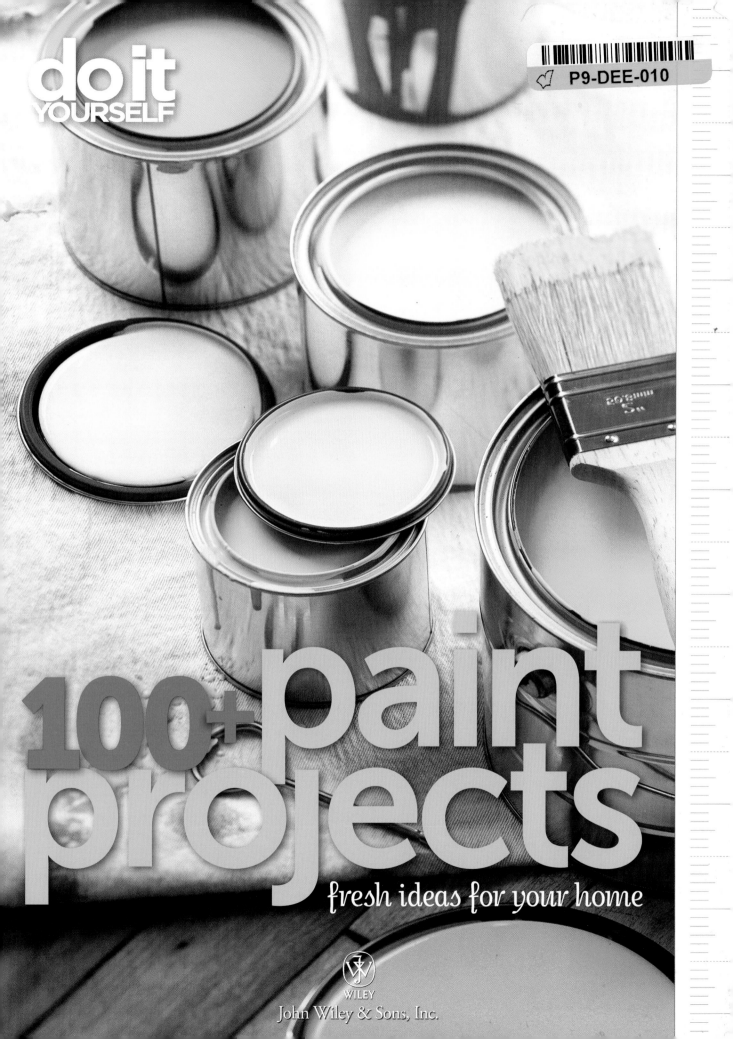

do it YOURSELF

P9-DEE-010

100+ paint projects

fresh ideas for your home

WILEY

John Wiley & Sons, Inc.

MEREDITH CORPORATION

Editorial Director
Gregory H. Kayko
Special Interest Media

Do It Yourself **Magazine Editors**
Bethany Kohoutek, Beth Eslinger

Do It Yourself **Magazine Art Directors**
Kimberly Metz,
Melissa Gansen Beauchamp

Contributing Book Editor
Pamela Porter

Contributing Book Designer
Angie Packer

Contributing Book Copy Editor
Elizabeth Keest Sedrel

Books Executive Editor
Larry Erickson

Group Editor
Lacey Howard

Deputy Content Director
Karman Hotchkiss

Art Director, Home Design
Gene Rauch

Administrative Assistant
Heather Knowles

**Contributing Designers &
Painters**
Meredith Ladik Drumond, Jodi
Mensing Harris, Cathy Kramer,
John Loecke, Patricia Mohr
Kramer, Patricia McClure, Mathew
Mead, Vicki Nail, Jean Schissel
Norman, Angie Packer, Pamela
Porter, Wade Sherrer, Jessica
Thomas, Connie Webb, Jeni
Wright

Contributing Photographers
Adam Albright, King Au, Marty
Baldwin, Monica Buck, Kim
Cornelison, Jason Donnelly, Bill
Hopkins, Steven MacDonald,
Mathew Mead, James Merrell,
Cameron Sadeghpour, Greg
Scheidemann, Jay Wilde

Note to the Readers:
Due to differing conditions, tools, and individual skills, John Wiley & Sons, Inc., assumes
no responsibility for any damages, injuries suffered, or losses incurred as a result of
following the information published in this book. Before beginning any project, review
the instructions carefully, and if any doubts or questions remain, consult local experts or
authorities. Because codes and regulations vary greatly, you always should check with
authorities to ensure that your project complies with all applicable local codes and
regulations. Always read and observe all of the safety precautions provided by
manufacturers of any tools, equipment, or supplies, and follow all accepted safety
procedures.

Ready, set, paint!

Whether furniture, floors, textiles, or tiles top your project list, there's no better DIY value than letting paint drive your redo. Paint is, after all, transformation in a can. And better yet, it's the quickest and thriftiest way we know of to refresh just about anything. That's why Team DIY would rather pick up a paintbrush than any other tool in the house. It's also why we've compiled our favorite DIY paint projects into this must-have, inspiring page-turner.

This book is divided into eight chapters. Chapters 1 through 6 feature paint treatments on different surfaces: Fabric & Textiles; Furniture; Walls and Floors; Artwork and Accessories; Ceramics, Glass & Metal; and Cabinetry & Tle. The indispensable Chapter 7—Tips, Tools & Techniques—is where you'll want to flip before popping open any can of paint. And if oodles of original patterns pique your interest, take a peek at Chapter 8. Be sure not to miss Sources and the oh-so-valuable "Project Index" at the back of the book.

Whew! With all this information in hand, you can roll, spray, brush, stamp, or stencil your way to fabulous, showstopping creations. And if you have your share of do-overs, don't despair. We've certainly had an oops now and then. But that's the beauty of paint— just let it dry, then try, try again.

Now, unleash the DIYer in you and get ready, get set, and paint your world!

— Team DIY

Do It Yourself | 100+ Paint Projects

do it YOURSELF

100+ paint projects

projects & how-tos

resources

For a road map of how to use this book, check out the Project Index on

PAGE 207

Chapter 1

PAINT PROJECTS FOR

fabric & textiles

stenciling

stamping

more ideas

PAGES 8–17   PAGES 18–25   PAGES 26–35

stencilling

If you can't find masking tape in the width needed, cut it using a rotary cutter on a self-healing mat or use car striping tape instead.

Blooming Beauty

LAYERING ADDS DELIGHTFUL DEPTH TO A PLUSH PILLOW.

With a few inexpensive supplies, you can make your own designer-style pillows in no time. Double the fun by using two painting techniques—layering one atop the other—to create a custom treasure that will cheer up a lonesome chair, sofa, or bed.

YOU'LL NEED:

_Fabric

_Scissors

_Masking tape

_Fabrics spray paint

_Stencil

_Stencil adhesive

_Stencil brush

_Acrylic crafts paint

_Sewing machine

_Thread

_Piping cord

_Pillow form

1. Wash and dry the fabric. From the fabric, cut the pillow front and back to the desired size. Apply strips of masking tape in a crisscross pattern along the entire width of the right side of the pillow front (**fig. a**).

2. Place the pillow front on a protected surface and spray with fabrics spray paint (**fig. b**). Let dry and remove the masking strips.

3. Secure the stencil to the fabric using stencil adhesive. Use a stencil brush to apply crafts paint with a straight up and down pouncing motion (**fig. c**). Let dry.

4. From the same fabric, sew a length of piping to fit around the pillow. Place the pillow front and back together with right sides facing and piping cord sandwiched in between. Sew around the perimeter, leaving an opening for turning. Turn, insert the pillow form, and hand-stitch the opening closed.

fig. a

fig. b

fig. c

THE PALETTE:
sunny side up

Drenched in vibrant colors, this palette is as cheerful as a spring day. Sunny yellow mixes with sky blue and punchy pink to create a garden of blooming hues.

Add an instant dose of warmth and cheer with a golden hue.

A bit of chartreuse green fits with almost any color scheme.

Turquoise is quite possibly the most perfect blue hue.

Kick things up a notch by adding hot pink to the mix.

Patterned Panels

LARGE-SCALE STENCILS MAKE A BIG IMPACT.

Give plain sailcloth curtains a big style lift with an arabesque design stenciled in chocolate brown.
The unexpected size of the stencil turns an otherwise traditional motif into a modern masterpiece.
To make the project easy and affordable, use latex paint and a roller to transfer the design.

YOU'LL NEED:

_Pattern

_Stencil plastic

_Kraft paper

_Pencil

_Curtain panels

_Ruler

_Painter's tape

_Stencil adhesive

_Foam roller

_Fabrics paint

_Paint tray

1. Make a stencil using the pattern on page 192 and stencil plastic. On a large work surface (we used a 4x8-foot sheet of plywood atop two sawhorses), lay out kraft paper the size of your curtain panel. Draw a vertical centerline, then trace your stencil pattern on the paper to find the best positioning for your pattern (**fig. a**).

2. Lay a washed and pressed curtain panel on the work surface. Find the vertical center of the panel with the ruler and apply a strip of painter's tape to the center.

3. Spray the stencil with the adhesive and place it on the curtain, starting with one of the centrally placed patterns. Using a stencil roller and a bit of paint, roll the paint over the pattern. Remove the stencil carefully.

4. Using the guide marks on the stencil's edges, align the pattern to repeat the stencil process. Repeat the pattern all over the curtain (**fig. b**).

diy tip

When stenciling on fabric, place a very small amount of paint in the tray and keep the roller fairly dry to prevent paint from bleeding. Practice on a scrap of fabric first.

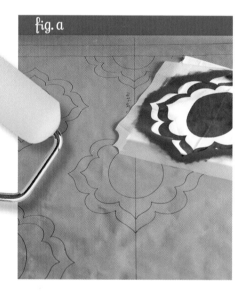
fig. a

fig. b

THE PALETTE:
sophisticated

Chocolate brown paired with cream anchors this sophisticated color scheme. A small dose of powder pink adds subtle interest without sacrificing elegance.

Barely-there pink is more powerful than you might think.

Pretty tan baskets add color and oh-so-important texture.

For the dominant hue, drench your space in rich brown.

Keep things fresh with contrasting creamy whites.

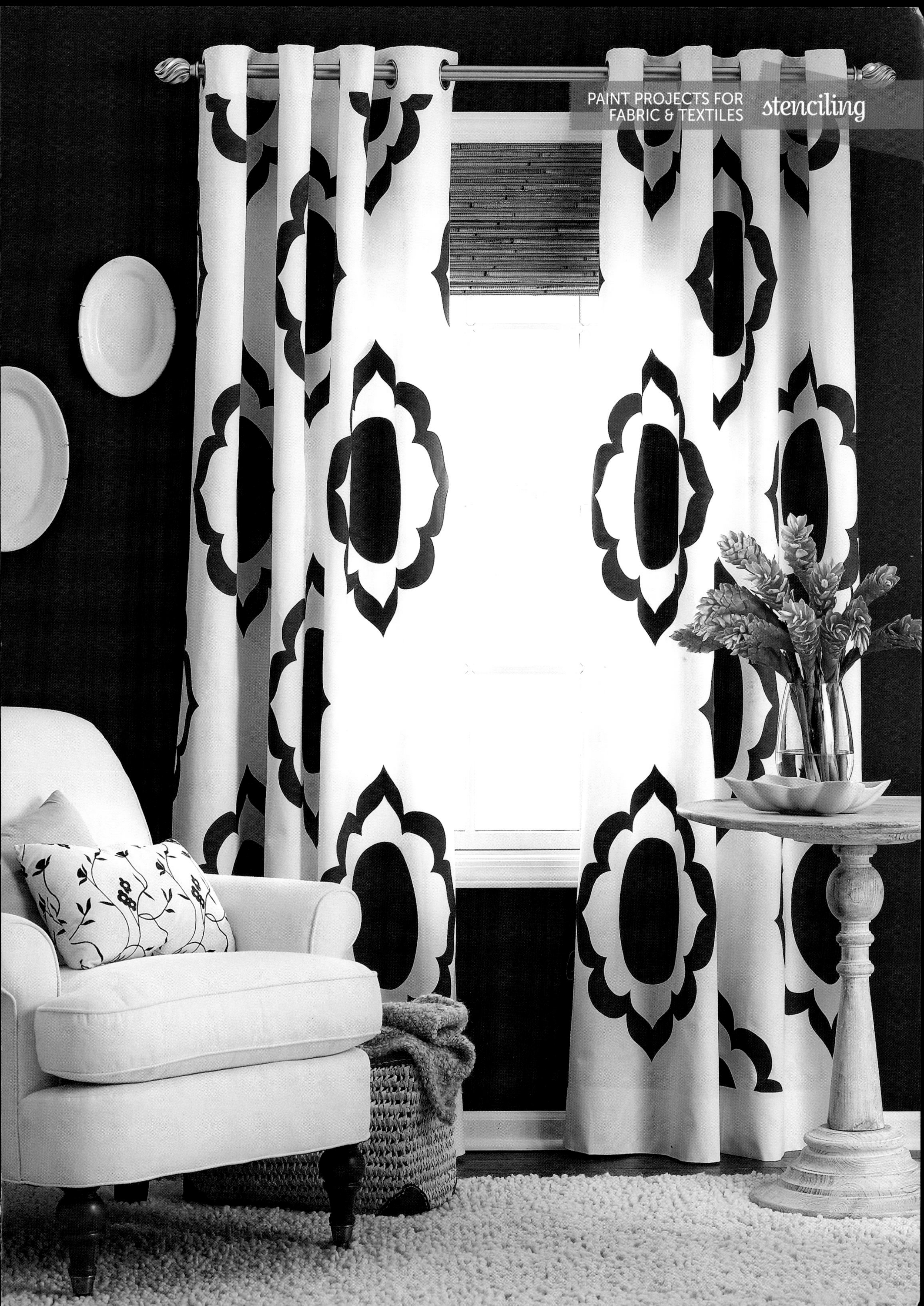

A Mixed Bag

CORRAL OFFICE CLUTTER IN A GRAFFITI-STYLE TOTE.

Tired of your plain princess pink tote? With a sassy stencil motif and cavalier handwork, even the perkiest hue can sport a little edge. So make your mark, then put that tote to use stowing books and files out of sight so your desk looks tidy.

YOU'LL NEED:

_Pencil

_Contact paper

_Scissors

_Canvas bag

_Fabrics spray paints

_Fabrics paint pens

1. Search online for an image of your favorite shoes—or snap a photo of those old-school kicks buried in the back of your closet. Bold, simple images work best. Trace the outline of the image on contact paper to make a stencil. Cut out the stencil, peel it from its backing, and adhere it to a tote bag, pressing securely.

2. Spray the design with a light coat of fabrics spray paint. Let dry. Apply a second light coat if you want a richer result **(fig. a)**.

3. Peel up the stencil **(fig. b)**.

4. Add more colors and layers by placing paper over parts of the design and respraying with the desired colors. White offers a nice background here, and notice the partially masked heart shape. Scrawl graffiti words with fabrics paint pens.

diy tip
When painting double-layer fabric items such as bags or T-shirts, place paper between the layers to keep the wet paint from sticking them together. It's also a good idea to wash the item before painting it to allow for any shrinkage.

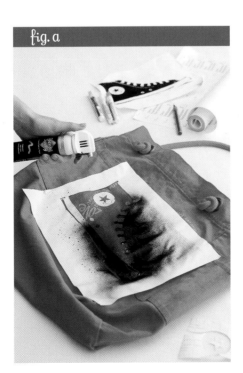

fig. a

fig. b

May I Have a Word?

A PAINTED MESSAGE SAYS IT ALL.

Let your table linens strike up a conversation by flaunting a playful word or phrase. Painted handwriting is an easy way to embellish a dull table runner or even cloth napkins while expressing yourself to dinner guests.

YOU'LL NEED:

_Sheet of paper

_Marker

_Masking tape

_Self-healing
 cutting mat

_Stencil acetate

_Crafts knife

_Purchased table
 runner or napkins

_Stencil adhesive

_Round stencil brush

_Acrylic paint

_Iron

1. Handwrite a word on a piece of paper with a thick marker. (Use the marker to further thicken parts of the letters, if needed.) Or if you don't love your handwriting, print letters using a pretty font on your computer or use the pattern on page 193.

2. Tape the word to a self-healing cutting mat and then tape a piece of clear acetate over the top. Use a crafts knife to cut out the letters (**fig. a**).

3. Select the perfect position for the word on the table runner or napkins. Tape the fabric to a protected work surface and adhere the stencil to the fabric using stencil adhesive. Use a round stencil brush to paint on the word, dabbing the paint evenly for a crisp, opaque result (**fig. b**).

4. If desired, heat-set using an iron.

diy tip

When using a stencil brush, keep the brush straight up and down or perpendicular to the stencil and use a quick pouncing motion to apply small amounts of paint. Build up coats for desired coverage.

fig. a

fig. b

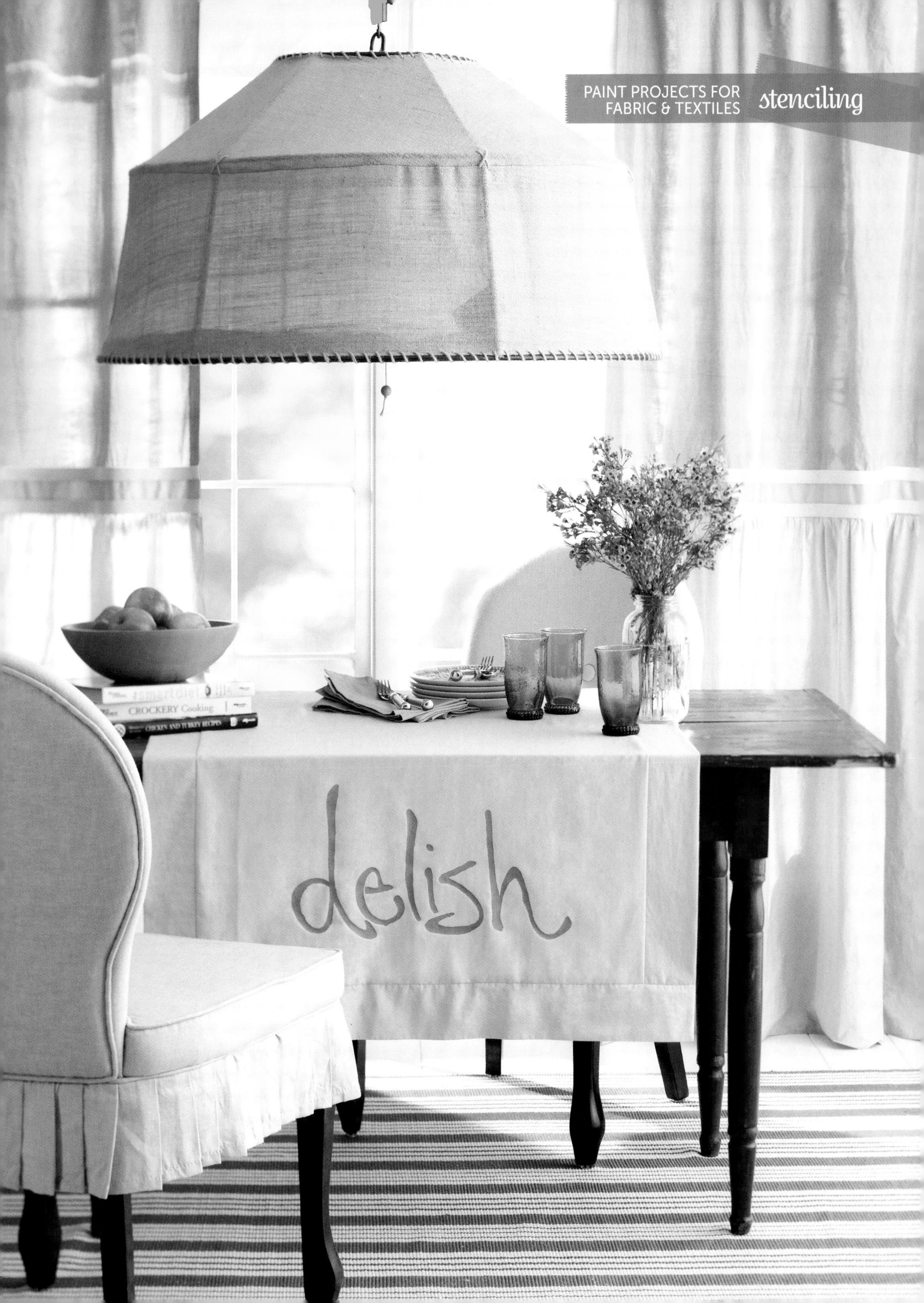
CROCKERY Cooking
delish

fig. a

In Full Bloom

FIND ELEGANCE IN A TONE-ON-TONE TREATMENT.

An oversized zinnia stencil gives off-the-rack curtains a custom look.

1. Position the stencil on the curtain and use stencil adhesive to secure it in place.

2. With kraft paper underneath to absorb excess paint, apply paint with a small crafts brush or stencil brush using a pouncing motion (**fig. a**).

3. Remove the stencil and reposition either randomly or in a predetermined pattern. Repeat the process.

Nature Calls

FRESHEN UP A ROOM WITH BOTANICAL SILHOUETTES.

Make a single pillow like this one, or a grouping of pillows sporting a variety of leaves.
Try mixing in other elements of nature such as birds, insects, or flowers.

YOU'LL NEED:

_Pillow

_Cardboard

_Leaf pattern

_Contact paper

_Masking tape

_Fabrics spray paint

_Scissors

1. Start with a beige or cream-color linen or cotton pillow. Remove the pillow form and insert cardboard into the pillowcase.

2. Create a large foliage stencil by enlarging the pattern on page 193 and printing or tracing it onto contact paper. Cut out and peel the backing from the paper and adhere to the pillow. Mask the edges of the pillow with masking tape.

3. Spray bright green fabrics paint over the stencil. Let dry and remove the contact paper.

stamping

To achieve this textured wood print effect, don't chip away every bit of the linoleum block surface.

Coming Up Roses

BOOST YOUR BEDROOM WITH A STUNNING STAMP.

A queen-size periwinkle sheet and pillowcase prove the perfect pair for this billowing canopy and accent pillow.

YOU'LL NEED:

_Rose pattern

_Marker

_Linoleum block

_Wood chisel

_Rubber brayer
  (roller)

_Acrylic paint

_Scissors

_Queen bedsheet
  and pillowcase

_Sewing machine

_Thread

_Coordinating fabric

_Ball fringe

_Plastic rings

_Cup hooks

_Pillow form

1. Copy and cut out the rose pattern on page 193. Use a marker to trace the pattern onto the top of a linoleum block. Draw an oversize dot on a second block (**fig. a**).

2. Using a wood chisel, carve away all the areas of the designs you don't want to print. The chisels come in different sizes to make quick work of large areas and carefully shape fine details (**fig. b**).

3. Roll the paint evenly onto the raised parts of the stamp block. You'll get only one print per roll of paint; try to reload with about the same amount of paint each time (**fig. c**).

4. Cut open the pillowcase. Tape down the sheet and open the case before stamping so they won't wrinkle or move. Then, firmly press and remove the stamp where you want the pattern to appear. Experiment with both even and uneven pressure as you stamp different areas (**fig. d**).

5. When dry, sew a border around the canopy and open case using coordinating fabric. Add ball fringe to both and sew the case into a pillow of the desired size and shape, inserting pillow form. Sew plastic rings to the canopy and hang them from cup hooks secured to the wall and ceiling.

fig. a

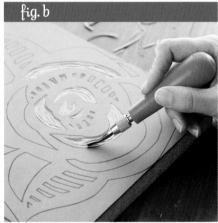
fig. b

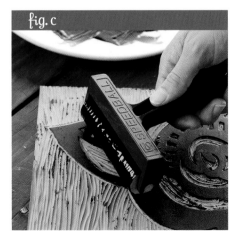
fig. c

fig. d

diy tip
When tracing an image on linoleum block, be sure to reverse it so it transfers correctly when you stamp it on your fabric or any other surface.

Catch of the Day

TREAT TEA TOWELS TO A FUN-FILLED BEACH MOTIF.

You don't need art school to make these smart little fish—simply carve a fishy shape onto a potato, then stamp away, changing colors for interest.

1. Cut a potato in half lengthwise. Size a pattern on page 193 to fit on the potato, then cut it out.

2. Flip over the cut pattern and place it on the potato. Using a chisel, carve around the perimeter of the pattern, cutting about ¼ inch deep. Remove the pattern and continue to chisel away the negative space around the motif as well as any details on the motif (**fig. a**).

3. Tap crafts paint onto the stamp using a stiff-bristle paintbrush. Tapping applies a more even coat than brushing. Then stamp your heart out (**fig. b**).

diy tip

If you're not confident of your artistic skills, use cookie cutters as patterns or copy our patterns on page 193.

fig. a

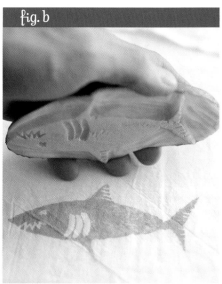

fig. b

THE PALETTE:
breath of fresh air

Shades of blue and green are a perfect choice for a sea-inspired space. These fresh greens and blues offer just the right amount of variety to keep the palette from being too predictable.

Let citrus green punch up a traditional seaside palette.

For any beachy scene, seafoam green is an essential choice.

Marine blue adds depth and richness to the airy palette.

You can't go wrong with basic blue—America's favorite hue.

When stamping heavy-use fabrics such as tea towels, mix paints with textile medium or use fabrics paints, both found at crafts stores.

Some new fabrics have a coating that may prevent paint from adhering. Washing removes the coating and allows the fabric to shrink before you apply your stamps.

Garden Party

THIS BLISSFUL BEDDING WILL LEAVE YOU DREAMING OF DAISIES.

While flowers work delightfully for this project, if you like to get creative, here's your chance. Experiment by using different objects as paint stamps. Think beyond flowers and fronds, move past potatoes and sponges—push your imagination and experiment a little.

YOU'LL NEED:

_Sheets and pillowcases

_Gerbera daisies

_Fabrics paint pens

_Ruler

_Paintbrush

_Washable fabrics
  paints

_Paper plate

_Cardboard

1. Wash and dry the sheets and pillowcases. Choose a flower for your stamp—gerbera daisies work well because they are relatively flat. Measure and plan the position of the stamps. Using a fabrics paint pen and ruler, draw a square to frame each flower stamp.

2. Brush a puddle of washable fabrics paint onto a paper plate or kraft paper, then dip the face of the flower into the paint (**fig. a**).

3. With cardboard underneath to prevent the paint from bleeding through, press the flower stamp onto the sheet in the center of each frame (**fig. b**).

4. Carefully remove the flower. Repeat in the desired colors and let dry (**fig. c**).

fig. a

fig. b

fig. c

THE PALETTE:
over the rainbow

A bouquet of hues blooms in this room. Choose your favorite hues or take cues from your flowers, making sure the colors share a similar value (the lightness or darkness of the color).

Periwinkle blue plays well with this mix of bright hues.

Bright pink works, or try a reddish raspberry hue.

A twist of lemon yellow offers sun-kissed freshness.

Juicy hues like this orange are ripe for this palette.

diy tip

When a fabric painting project is dry, heat-setting with an iron fixes the paint to the fabric. Be sure to follow the paint manufacturer's instructions to heat-set.

fig. a

Hip to Be Square

GEOMETRIC SHAPES MAKE MODERN STYLE EASY.

Basic squares are the building blocks for this curtain transformation.

YOU'LL NEED:

_Wood block

_Crafts foam

_Spray adhesive

_Foam brush

_Fabrics paints

_Iron

1. Buy a wood block in your desired size or use a scrap of wood. Trace around the block onto a sheet of crafts foam. Cut out the foam and use spray adhesive to secure to the block.

2. Use a foam brush or roller to apply fabrics paint to the stamp. Once coated, press the stamp onto the curtain panel with even pressure, then lift off carefully (**fig. a**).

3. Finish stamping your design, cleaning your stamp before each new color. Heat-set if desired.

Take a Seat

STAMP A BOUQUET OF ROSES.

This quick and easy project will have you sitting pretty in no time. Follow the directions on page 19 for linoleum block stamping and use the rose pattern on page 193. Stamp onto a purchased fabric-covered seat cushion or onto one you cover with fabric yourself. Stamping on fabric first and then trying to stretch it over a seat makes it more difficult to position your design where desired.

YOU'LL NEED:

_Rose pattern

_Linoleum block

_Linoleum cutter

_Paint roller

_Fabrics paints

_Fabric seat cushion

The first impression of the stamp may not be the best, so stamp first on a piece of paper to remove excess paint, then stamp on your project.

more ideas

Use fabrics markers to make this coordinating accent pillow adorned with freehand scribble-style flowers.

Into the Woods
MIMIC TREE BARK WITH FREEHAND DOODLES.

Two products make this wood-grain-effect curtain embellishment super simple: wide sponge-tip fabrics markers such as Tee Juice brand and bottled fabrics paint with narrow-tip applicators such as Scribbles brand.

YOU'LL NEED:

_Curtain panels

_Drop cloth

_Pencil

_Tee Juice markers

_Scribbles fabrics paint

1. Wash and dry the curtain panels. Lay the panels out on a large work surface protected with a drop cloth to prevent the paint from bleeding through. Draw a wood-grain design lightly with a pencil, then draw over the lines with a Tee Juice fabrics marker (**fig. a**).

2. Fill in with fine lines using Scribbles bottled paint (**fig. b**). Keep the lines loose to achieve a hand-done effect, which means you simply can't make a mistake with this project!

diy tip
Linen, cotton, and natural-fiber fabrics absorb paint best. As with all paint products, read the package instructions to ensure the best outcome.

fig. a

fig. b

THE PALETTE:
down to earth

Earthy hues give this room a retro woodland feel. Team browns, greens, and yellows. Then throw things just a little off course with a touch of rusty red or unexpected royal blue.

Just a small dose of brown goes a long way in this scheme.

The great outdoors wouldn't be complete without mossy green.

Avoid utter darkness by substituting mustard yellow for brown.

Across the color wheel, royal blue throws a nice curve in the mix.

Let's Face It

CAT-EYE GLASSES GIVE THIS PILLOW RETRO VOGUE.

If your DIY ambition has always stopped at giving screen printing a try, this lovely lady motif ought to tempt you to step out of your comfort zone. The method is a simplified version of traditional screen printing, so give it a shot.

YOU'LL NEED:

_Face pattern

_Contact paper

_Scissors

_Screen-printing
 screen

_Cotton fabric

_Masking tape

_Textile ink or screen-
 printing paint

_Squeegee

1. Use the face pattern on page 194 or download a pattern online. Enlarge to the desired size of the finished pillow and trace the pattern onto contact paper. Cut out the pieces you don't want to be painted. Peel the backing from the contact paper pieces and stick them to the flat side of a screen-printing screen from a crafts store. For this pillow, white ink is applied over black fabric so all black sections of the pillow were masked with contact paper pieces applied to the screen.

2. Cut cotton fabric to the desired size and secure to a protected work surface using masking tape. Position the screen on the fabric with the contact paper sandwiched between the screen and the fabric.

3. Spoon textile ink or screen-printing paint across the top of the screen, spreading evenly. Use a squeegee to draw the paint down over the entire screen and back up again (**fig. a**).

4. Lift the screen carefully to reveal your design (**fig. b**). Let dry, then sew into a pillow.

diy tip

This contact paper method works well for beginners and for simple designs. It also allows you to easily reuse your screen again and again. Flip to page 30 for another easy-do screen printing technique.

fig. a

fig. b

Mr. Roboto

WELCOME A LITTLE GEEK CHIC TO THE TABLE.

Prepare to flash back to elementary school art class, because you may feel like a second-grader while doing this project. In fact, if you've got kids, let them join the fun.

YOU'LL NEED:

_Fabrics marker

_Robot pattern

_Cloth napkin

_Elmer's School Glue Gel

_Crafts brush

_White fabrics paint

_Pan

_Warm water

_Iron

1. Use a disappearing fabrics marker to trace the robot pattern from page 194 (or download another motif online) onto a colorful cloth napkin. Use Elmer's School Glue Gel and a crafts brush to mask the areas you don't want to paint **(fig. a)**. Let dry.

2. Paint a circle over the design using white fabrics paint; let dry.

3. Soak the napkin in a pan of warm water for 10 minutes to dissolve the glue gel. Use a washcloth to gently rub the glue gel from the fabric, revealing your design **(fig. b)**. Heat-set, following the paint manufacturer's instructions, if desired.

fig. a

fig. b

THE PALETTE:
candy colors

Perfect for kids' rooms or family spaces, this anything-goes mix of happy hues is sweet as pie. These are just a few of the tasty colors that work in this palette.

Turquoise is a treat that helps ground the playful palette.

Bring out your inner kid with sassy sour apple green.

Tart and true, lemon drop yellow is a smiley hue.

Grape is a favorite flavor and color welcome at any table.

Screenplay

SIMPLIFIED WITH CRAFTS GLUE, THIS ONE'S A MUST-DO!

Screen printing isn't just for artsy T-shirts. Use this fast and fun technique to punch up pillows or trick out an ordinary tote bag.

YOU'LL NEED:

_Screen-printing
 screen

_Soft lead pencil

_Paintbrush

_Mod Podge

_Pillow or tote bag

_Textile ink or screen-
 printing paint

_Squeegee

1. Create a design by printing clip art or text or by drawing a simple shape on paper. Set the design on your work surface and position a screen-printing screen facedown on top. Lightly trace the design using a soft lead pencil so you don't rip the screen (**fig. a**).

2. Flip over the frame so the screen is facing up. Brush Mod Podge onto the areas of your design that you don't want to be printed. Let dry. Check for small holes by holding the screen up to a light. Any place where light shines through will be printed. Smear more Mod Podge on any area where light shines through (**fig. b**).

3. Place the item to be screen-printed on a level work surface and smooth or iron out wrinkles. Position the frame screen-side down on top of the item. Pour ink or paint along the upper inside of the screen above the pattern, then pull it down the screen with a squeegee held at a 45-degree angle (**fig. c**). Lift the screen and let the project dry.

4. Gently rinse the screen with tap water. Do not use soap or scrubbing tools. Let the screen air-dry so you can reuse it.

diy tip
If you're printing words, they'll look backward from the front of the screen, but they'll print correctly when done.

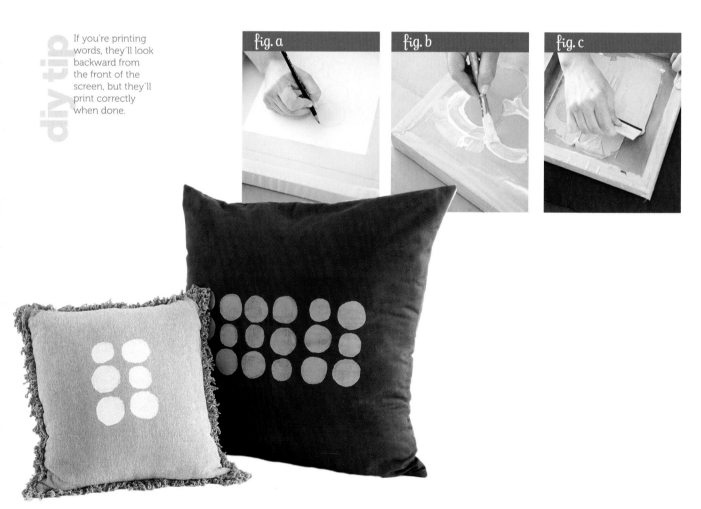

fig. a

fig. b

fig. c

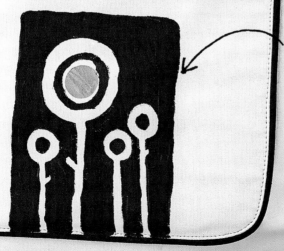

Find this flower pattern on page 194. Use a second screen for the blue dot or hand-paint the easy shape when the screened design is dry.

Table Toppers

THIS PLAYFUL TABLESCAPE IS READY FOR ANY PARTY.

Fun-filled designs give table linens a reason to celebrate. Look for tightly woven, smooth textiles, which are highly absorbent and accept paint easily.

1. Trace and cut out the flower pattern from page 194.

2. Tape the place mat faceup on a protected work surface. Over the place mat, layer tracing paper, plain paper (to prevent tracing paper ink from bleeding onto the pattern), and the pattern. Tape the pattern in place.

3. Using a pencil, trace the pattern, repositioning the tracing paper as necessary. Remove all papers.

4. Fill in the design elements using fabrics paint and a stiff-bristle brush. Use an angle shader to fill in points and sharpen edges. Use the dauber to fill in circles. Let the paint dry.

5. Apply additional coats of paint to achieve the desired look, then heat-set the paint following the paint manufacturer's directions.

6. To create the confetti pattern on the flower center and napkin, simply dab on paint with the tip of a brush.

Pillow Talk

IN A WORD, THIS PROJECT IS A MUST.

As luck would have it, this pillow is a snap to make—and quite a conversation piece. The hardest part just might be selecting the right word or phrase to paint. So take an evening and say what's on your mind.

YOU'LL NEED:

_Fabric

_Scissors

_Paintbrush

_Dressmaker's carbon
  transfer paper

_Clear gesso medium

_Fabrics paint

_Sewing machine

_Thread

_Piping cord

_Pillow form

1. From the fabric, cut the pillow front and back to the desired size. Print or photocopy letters. Using the end of a paintbrush as a stylus, trace letters onto the pillow front using dressmaker's carbon transfer paper (or tracing paper as described for the project on page 34).

2. Paint gesso inside the transferred lines and let dry (**fig. a**).

3. Paint fabrics paint over the gesso; let dry (**fig. b**). Machine-stitch around the letters.

4. Cut piping to fit around the perimeter of the pillow and cover with fabric cut on the bias. Place the pillow front and back together with right sides facing and piping sandwiched in between. Sew together, leaving an opening. Turn, insert the pillow form, and hand-stitch the opening closed.

fig. a

fig. b

Chapter 2

PAINT PROJECTS FOR

furniture

stenciling

masking

stamping

more ideas

PAGES 38–45   PAGES 46–51   PAGES 52–55   PAGES 56–69

stenciling

diy tip

Cutting a stencil from flexible frisket paper or film (found at most art supply stores) makes it easier to stencil around corners and curves. Because this material is less durable, you may need to make duplicate stencils if your pattern requires many repeats.

Wake-Up Call

WITH ITS BOLD PATTERN, THIS BED SHOUTS RISE AND SHINE.

A classic houndstooth pattern inspired this color-charged bed frame. Stretching floor to ceiling, the canopy and turned posts made the piece a little tricky to stencil, but the end result is anything but sleepy.

YOU'LL NEED:

_Primer

_Orange and red
  latex paint

_Houndstooth
  pattern

_Stencil film

_Crafts knife

_Pencil

_Ruler

_Stencil adhesive

_Paint roller

_Burnishing tool

1. Prime the bed frame and paint a base coat in the lighter orange color. Paint the canopy frame and posts in the darker red color (**fig. a**). Let dry.

2. Enlarge and photocopy the houndstooth pattern on page 195. Trace onto stencil film and cut out. With a pencil and ruler, mark a horizontal grid around the bed frame to guide placement of the stencil.

3. Choose a starting point and use stencil adhesive to adhere the stencil to the bed. Fill in the shape with the red color using a small paint roller. Carefully reposition the stencil while the paint is still wet. Continue until the frame, headboard, and footboard are complete. Let dry.

4. To add pattern to the posts and sides (**fig. b**), carefully wrap the stencil around the edges and curves. Run a credit card or burnishing tool over the stencil to avoid any gaps. Fill in. Let dry.

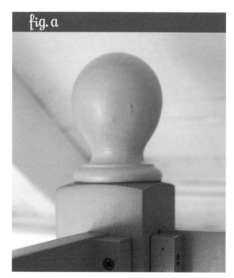
fig. a

fig. b

THE PALETTE:
the heat is on

Reds and oranges blaze the way for this sizzling color scheme. Breezy white and cool blue keep things from getting too hot.

Orange sets the tone for this wonderfully warm bedroom.

A flickering bold color, this flame red claims the spotlight.

It only takes a splash of watery blue to cool this palette down.

White bedding and walls offer eyes a much-needed color break.

Feather Your Nest

FOR A SUBTLE STATEMENT, USE A TONE-ON-TONE APPLICATION.

This flock of birds finds the perfect perch on a vintage dining table cut down to coffee table height.

YOU'LL NEED:

_Primer

_Light and dark red
  latex paint

_Bird stencil

_Stencil adhesive

_Stencil brush

1. Prime, then paint the table using flat or satin paint in a light red hue. Let dry. Secure the stencil using stencil adhesive and fill in using a stencil brush and dark red paint. Move the stencil, using the registration marks to line up the next position.

2. Complete one half of the table with the stencil running one way, then turn the stencil 180 degrees to complete the other half of the table. That way the birds are right side up on both of the drop leaves. Let dry (**fig. a**).

3. Let easy-to-make art plaques complete your space. Simply stencil part of the bird design on four small pieces of painted plywood (**fig. b**).

fig. a

fig. b

THE PALETTE:
bohemian

Vibrant and chic, this attention-getting palette is artsy and intense, yet it's one that even a conservative decorator can love.

Ripe with orange-red hues, this room is sassy yet serene.

Even a small dose of bright red sparks drama and attitude.

Lush and lively, green is easy to add to most schemes.

This palette wouldn't be complete without passionate purple.

Outlining the recessed edge in dark red accentuates the table's pretty shape.

Center Stage

TWO HUES MAKE THIS MOTIF MAGNIFICENT.

Flaunting a single center medallion, this petite piece shows that even the tiniest table can showcase a sensational stencil.

YOU'LL NEED:

_Stencil

_Spray adhesive

_Stencil brush

_Semigloss tan and gray crafts paints

_Paper towels

1. Measure the surface and find a stencil to fit. Secure the stencil to the tabletop using a stencil spray adhesive.

2. Lightly dip a stencil brush into tan paint, dab off the excess on a paper towel, and, using a pouncing motion, brush in the areas of the stencil you want to be tan (**fig. a**). Repeat with gray paint in the areas you want to be gray. Remove the stencil and let dry.

fig. a

The washed highlights of the wood grain under the stencil add fun texture and dimension.

As an alternative to stencils like this, try decorative vinyl decals for a quick and easy embellishment.

Custom Details

BOOST A BLAND BROWN DRESSER.

Though darn cheap, this brown assemble-it-yourself dresser was an eyesore before being transformed with a bit of paint.

YOU'LL NEED:

_Stencil adhesive

_Die cut motif

_Paint roller

_Primer

_White semigloss
  latex paint

1. Use stencil adhesive to secure a crafts store die cut to the dresser, cutting as needed to jump from one drawer to another.

2. Roll a primer and two coats of white semigloss paint over the drawers, letting it dry between coats.

3. Carefully peel away the die cut mask, revealing the intricate, unpainted design underneath.

Jungle Love
ADD A TOUCH OF TROPICAL STYLE.

If a trip to the tropics isn't in your foreseeable future, bring a bit of paradise home with a facade of fabulous fronds. Stenciled on an artist's canvas from the crafts store, the leaves are rendered in three green hues.

YOU'LL NEED:

_Leaf stencil

_Stencil brush

_Three green crafts
 paints

_Artist's canvas

1. Using a leaf stencil and stencil brush, apply one leaf color to the canvas; let dry. To add another color, reposition the stencil, slightly overlapping the first. Repeat for the second and third colors.

2. Turn the canvas into a door for an open bookcase by screwing on hinges and a painted wooden knob.

diy tip

In addition to using different colors, look for leaf stencils in a few different sizes or flip the stencil once in a while to vary motif.

fig. a

fig. b

diy tip
It's best to apply the paint in two or three thin layers rather than one thicker one, but there's no need to allow the paint to dry completely between coats.

Dining Delight
UNIQUE STENCILING GIVES THIS HUTCH NEW DIMENSION.

Creative positioning of stencils is what makes the hutch design one-of-a-kind. Notice how the cherry blossoms seem to grow right up the back of the hutch and over the doors.

1. Base-coat the hutch with semigloss paint; let it dry. Spray a thin coat of stencil adhesive on the back of the stencil (**fig. a**) and position the stencil on the hutch.

2. Lightly dip a stencil brush into paint, dab off the excess on a paper towel, and brush in the open areas of the stencil using a pouncing motion (**fig. b**).

3. Work from the inside of the stencil toward the outside, making sure the stencil is stuck down tightly so the paint won't bleed under.

4. Carefully remove the stencil and reposition it, or choose another of the stencils in the set, and continue stenciling until you have a grouping of motifs that you like. Remember, you can use the stencils upside down, backward, or any way that suits your design.

YOU'LL NEED:

_Semigloss paints

_Stencils

_Stencil adhesive

_Stencil brush

_Paper towels

It's a Fine Line

LET STRIPES DELIGHT AT DINNERTIME.

Colors in the curtain panels inspired the pink, brown, and green stripes sprucing up this once-plain dining table. Varying the stripe widths makes the piece even more playful.

YOU'LL NEED:

_Primer

_Latex paint

_Paintbrush and roller

_Pencil

_Measuring tape

_Level

_Painter's tape in
 ½-, 1-, 1½-, and
 2-inch widths

_Decorator's glaze

1. Prime the table. Let dry. Paint the table white. Let dry.

2. Using a pencil, measuring tape, and level, locate the center of the tabletop and mark off a wide centered stripe. Tape along the lines using 1-inch painter's tape. Measure 2 inches over from each length of tape and mark the length of the table. Run the tape along these lines. Brush decorator's glaze over the taped edges to seal. Let dry.

3. Paint brown between the first strips of tape to create the wide center stripe. Paint green between the second strips of tape to create the narrower parallel stripes. Remove the tape and let dry.

4. Repeat these steps along the side and around the legs of the table using different widths of tape to vary the stripes as desired (**fig. a**).

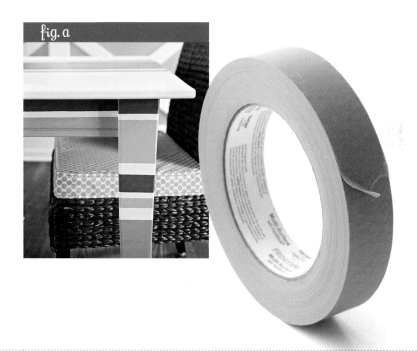

fig. a

div tip If the paint starts to pull off in a jagged line when you remove the tape, carefully score along the tape edge using a utility knife.

THE PALETTE:
playful melody

Rooted in deep brown tones, this scheme starts off serious. But a not-so-grown-up side shows through with the addition of perky pink and green hues.

Yummy chocolate brown drenches the room in richness.

Fresh and serene, green adds a touch of the great outdoors.

A dose of salmon pink is what gives the palette its subtle spark.

Creamy white keeps the scheme from becoming too chaotic.

Dresser Redo

FALLING LEAVES BRING A BIT OF NATURE INSIDE.

Don't settle for boring drawers when a lively facelift is quick, easy, and affordable. The large leaf silhouette is repeated to create a modern showpiece.

YOU'LL NEED:

_Leaf pattern

_Pencil

_Repositionable
 adhesive vinyl

_Scissors

_Paint roller

_Acrylic matte
 medium

_Green latex paint

_Crafts brush

1. Using a reverse stencil technique, enlarge the leaf pattern on page 195 to the desired size. Trace onto repositionable adhesive vinyl (from a signmaker's shop), then cut out. Make as many vinyl leaves as you need, flipping the image on a few to add variety.

2. Adhere the leaves to the drawer fronts, cutting as needed to jump from drawer to drawer.

3. Use a small paint roller to apply a thin coat of acrylic matte medium to the drawer fronts. Let dry. Apply several thin coats of a green top coat in semigloss latex paint. Let dry.

4. Carefully remove the vinyl leaves, using a utility knife on stubborn edges. Touch up the edges with green paint and a small crafts brush if needed.

YOU'LL NEED:

_Primer

_Paint roller

_Latex paint in red
 and white

_Contact paper

_Crafts brush

The Great Divide
FURNITURE FACELIFTS DON'T GET MUCH EASIER THAN THIS.

Polka dots make an easy perk-up of this old wooden room divider. If you can cut a few circles and roll on paint, this makeover is right for you.

1. Prime the divider and let dry; then paint white and let dry.

2. Cut imperfect circles from contact paper and apply to the divider. Paint red and remove the circles when the paint is partially dry. Let dry completely, then touch up as needed using a crafts brush.

Striped Right

LET A RAINBOW OF COLORS DELIGHT A DECK OR PATIO.

This square, clean-lined chair is a perfect fit for a modern stripe pattern. The precise stripes on this chair were marked with painter's tape, then each section was spray-painted. For a quicker but less perfect stripe result, you can paint freehand, following the line of the weave.

YOU'LL NEED:

_Spray primer

_Painter's tape

_Newspaper

_Red outdoor spray paint

_Yellow, blue, green, orange, and white outdoor crafts paints

_Crafts brush

_Spray varnish

1. Prepare the wicker following the DIY tip on page 52.

2. Prime the chair; let dry. Use painter's tape and old newspaper to mask off the chair seat bottom and back. Base-coat the unmasked portion with red outdoor spray paint. Let dry.

3. Mask off and paint each stripe, allowing the paint to dry before painting the adjacent stripe. If desired, highlight each stripe with a mix of its base coat color plus white. Allow to dry and spray varnish if desired.

diy tip
To create more interest and dimension, position the pineapple pieces off-center and allow them to continue over the table edge and onto the sides. Because it's flexible, adhesive shelf paper easily folds over edges to achieve this look.

Fruit Punch

A PINEAPPLE TABLETOP IS QUITE THE CONVERSATION PIECE.

Let an oversize pineapple motif—a universal sign of hospitality—give dinner guests a big welcome.

YOU'LL NEED:

_Paint roller

_Ivory flat latex paint

_Pineapple pattern

_Adhesive shelf paper

_Orange semigloss
  paint

1. Paint the table ivory using flat latex paint. Using the pattern on page 196, cut the pineapple pieces from adhesive shelf paper. Arrange the pieces and stick down on the tabletop.

2. Paint the table using an orange semigloss hue. When dry, peel off the shelf paper to reveal the pineapple.

diy tip Before painting wicker furniture, prep it by vacuuming surfaces and crevices to remove dirt and scrubbing with a brush dipped in bleach water. Let dry, then smooth with fine-grade sandpaper, wipe with tack cloth, and spray with primer.

Wicker Wonders

WOVEN CASTOFFS FLAUNT FRESH NEW FACES.

Polka dots in various sizes and colors liven up a petite wicker chair rescued from the curb. The circular pattern mimics the curves of the seat and chair back. The flower chair and table enjoy a similar stamped treatment.

YOU'LL NEED:

_Spray primer

_Green and yellow
  outdoor spray paint

_Circle and flower
  patterns

_Crafts knife and
  self-healing mat

_Adhesive-back
  foam

_Clear Plexiglas

_Crafts brush

_Crafts paints in
  desired colors

_Spray varnish

Prepare the wicker following the DIY tip on the opposite page. Base-coat the primed furnishings with the desired color spray paint. Let dry. Using the patterns on page 195, cut circles and flowers from adhesive-back foam and mount to the Plexiglas. Use a crafts brush to apply paint to the foam stamp, then press the stamps on the chairs and ottoman. Allow to dry and varnish as desired.

Petal Pusher

A SOLID-BACK CHAIR BEGS FOR AN EMBELLISHMENT.

This starburst flower motif is an easy and appealing stamp to create, as are initials or modern geometric shapes. Find a design that works well in your room.

YOU'LL NEED:

_Flower pattern

_Pencil

_Adhesive foam
  sheets

_Crafts knife

_Cutting mat

_Clear Plexiglas

_Crafts paints

_Plastic plates

_Small foam
  paintbrushes

_Polyurethane

1. Using the pattern on page 195, make two photocopies of the flower. Be sure the copies are at the desired size and in reverse since the stamp will be the mirror image of the pattern.

2. Keep one copy as a placement guide and cut out pattern pieces from the second (**fig. a**).

3. Trace the patterns onto foam, numbering on the back if needed to keep pieces in the order you want. Cut the pieces from the foam using a crafts knife (**fig. b**).

4. Place clear Plexiglas over the pattern-placement guide, and secure the foam pieces in place to create your stamp (**fig. c**).

5. Pour paint on a plate and use small foam brushes to apply all paint colors to the stamp (**fig. d**). Turn the stamp over and press onto the surface. Let dry, then apply a protective coat of polyurethane.

fig. a

fig. b

fig. c

fig. d

Stamp the edges of a tablecloth and curtains to coordinate elements in a room.

Let colorful floral bedding, fabric, or wallpaper inspire your painted motif.

Budding Beauty

WHY PAINT A BED OF ROSES WHEN A SINGLE BLOOM WILL DO?

Dreaming of an eye-popping headboard like this? You can do it! Cut an arched shape from medium density fiberboard (MDF), then paint your heart out following these steps.

YOU'LL NEED:

_Primer

_Trim brush

_White satin latex paint

_Pencil

_Ruler

_Painter's tape

_Water-base sealer

_Crafts paints in dark pink, light pink, turquoise, white, brown, light green

_½-inch foam spouncer

_Flower pattern

_Tracing paper

_Graphite transfer paper

_Artist's brushes

1. Prime the headboard and let dry; then paint white and let dry.

2. Use a pencil and ruler to mark a ½-inch border 2 inches from the headboard edge. Mask lines using painter's tape. Apply water-base sealer along the taped edges to keep paint from bleeding under. When dry, paint between the tape using brown crafts paint. For dots, mark 1 inch from the headboard edge and 1½ inches between the dots. Use a foam spouncer to apply dots (**fig. a**).

3. Enlarge the pattern on page 197 to desired size and trace on tracing paper. Transfer the pattern to the headboard using graphite transfer paper. Paint in the desired colors using **fig. b** as a guide. When dry, apply two coats of water-base sealer.

fig. a

fig. b

THE PALETTE:
getting fresh

This dream scheme evokes a crisp, clean vibe customary of modern European style.

Cherry red is a cheery topping to this sweet mix.

Sky blue hands red the cool contrast that defines this scheme.

Lots of pure white is needed to put the fresh in this palette.

Small but mighty dashes of chartreuse make a big impact.

Crowning Touch

THE RIGHT TOOL MAKES THIS PROJECT EASY-DO.

Give a vintage dresser sweet new style with a fresh coat of paint and new glass knobs. But then treat the top to a faux bois wood-grain finish—it's the icing on the cake.

YOU'LL NEED:

_Paint roller

_Primer

_Turquoise and
  white latex paint

_Painter's tape

_Plastic container

_Glaze medium

_Paper plate

_Foam roller

_Wood-graining tool

_Finish sealer

1. Prime the dresser and let dry. Paint the dresser turquoise. When dry, use painter's tape to mask off the dresser top.

2. In the plastic container, mix 4 parts glaze medium with 1 part white paint. You'll need enough glaze to equal the amount of one coat of base color to cover the dresser top. Pour the glaze mixture on a paper plate (**fig. a**) and, using the foam roller, roll a narrow width of it on the dresser.

3. Working quickly, start at one side and pull the wood-graining tool across the dresser, creating a plank effect (**fig. b**). As you pull the tool, rock it back and forth to vary the texture. After one pass, repeat to make a second "plank" that slightly overlaps the first.

4. Continue across the entire dresser top, reloading the tool with the glaze mixture and cleaning the excess glaze from the tool as you go. Remove the tape and let dry. Apply two coats of finish sealer. Let dry, then top with your favorite accessories.

diy tip Wood-graining tools like this come in different widths to suit a variety of projects. Shake things up by alternating wide and narrow tools on the same surface.

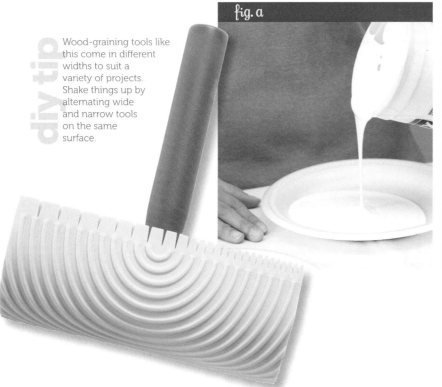

fig. a

fig. b

Don't be discouraged by color mistakes. This table was stained blue and painted gray before trying on this perfect spring green hue.

Pick Your Patina

A METALLIC TOP GIVES THIS REMAKE LOTS OF LUSTER.

Bright paint, silver leaf, and charming curtains (**fig. a**) breathe new life into a plain console turned cheery cottage buffet. Choose from a number of leafing and glazing products to achieve the gleaming finish you desire.

YOU'LL NEED:

_Sandpaper

_Primer

_Paint

_Paintbrush

_Mona Lisa adhesive, silver leaf, sealer, and antiquing glaze

_Waxed paper

_Fabric or café curtains

_Ribbon

_Tension rods

1. Sand, prime, and paint the table. Rough up the edges with sandpaper for a weathered look.

2. Apply adhesive to the tabletop and let sit for 30 minutes. Place a square piece of waxed paper over the silver leaf and run your hand over the waxed paper. Static electricity will cause the silver leaf to stick to the paper. Carefully place the two sheets onto the tacky surface. Rub the waxed paper and gently lift to separate it from the silver leaf. Repeat this step, slightly overlapping the edges of the silver leaf. When the entire surface is covered, use a dry paintbrush to burnish the silver leaf tight to the table and clean up loose edges.

3. Apply a coat of silver leaf sealer; let dry. Use a paintbrush to apply silver leaf antiquing glaze; let dry. To finish, apply a final coat of sealer (**fig. b**).

4. For the curtains, use store-bought café curtains or make your own by sewing a rod pocket in fabric or tea towels. Embellish with a ribbon or a strip of scrap fabric. Hang the curtains between the table legs using tension rods.

diy tip

Antiquing glaze gives this silver leaf a golden, aged finish. If you want a different look on your tabletop, try a different glaze or leaf.

fig. a

fig. b

THE PALETTE:

going coastal

Cheerful chartreuse kicks seaside hues up a notch in this boisterous beachy space.

Yellow-greens set the scene for a lively yet relaxed palette.

A touch of darker green helps tone the scheme down.

A beach cottage staple, seaglass blue is right at home.

Natural hues and textures are a must for this pretty palette.

Asian Flavor

LACQUERED RED OFFERS A FINISH THAT'S OUT OF THIS WORLD.

A drive to the local home improvement store turns out globe-trotting style for this writing desk. A black border and a coat of wax give the table an antique style.

YOU'LL NEED:

_Primer

_Paint and paintbrush

_Sharpie marker

_Briwax Original
  finishing wax

_Rag

_Wooden brackets

_Wood glue

_High-gloss
  polyurethane

1. Prime the table; let dry. Apply paint; let dry.

2. Using a Sharpie marker, outline the table's edges, then apply Briwax Original finishing wax with a rag to create an aged patina (**fig. a**).

3. Repeat these steps with unfinished decorative brackets, then attach to the table corners using wood glue (**fig. b**). For additional shine, apply several coats of high-gloss polyurethane.

diy tip

Pay attention to detail when working on your design. This could have been a plain painted desk, but the black Sharpie marker lines on the edges give it exceptional Asian flair.

fig. a

fig. b

THE PALETTE:
global views

Think across the ocean and try a mix of colors common to our Far Eastern friends. Who knows? A culture change just might suit you.

Red means luck and good fortune in Chinese culture.

Black is a defining hue, adding formality and flair.

Serene blue is the perfect canvas, letting bolder colors shine.

A staple in Asian design, natural hues help anchor this mix.

ART HISTORY   Marilyn Stokstad

Tord Boontje   Martina Margetts

Better than Leather

GET THE LOOK WITHOUT THE COST.

Inspired by the leather handles, this dresser goes formal with a sleek brown finish and handmade
"stitching" drawn with a gold-leaf pen.

YOU'LL NEED:

_Bondo adhesive

_Primer and paint

_Paintbrush

_Gold-leaf pen

_Ruler

_Leather pulls

_Drill and drill bits

1. Patch any drawer holes with Bondo adhesive.

2. Prime the dresser, let dry, and then paint with a satin-finish chocolate brown matched to the color of the leather pulls (**fig. a**). Pull out the drawers and paint all of the edges and sides.

3. Add stitches (**fig. b**) by drawing dashed lines using a gold-leaf pen and following a ruler for exact straight lines. Repeat around the top and the drawers. Use a damp towel to clean up any mistakes.

4. To secure the pulls, measure new holes for the leather handles and attach the hardware with a drill, following the philosophy "measure twice, cut once."

diy tip
For a scratch-resistant finish, apply two coats of clear polyurethane to the dresser, letting it dry and sanding lightly between coats.

fig. a

fig. b

Almost Antique

ADD INSTANT AGE WITH ANTIQUING GLAZE.

Trim molding added to the drawer fronts and a set of antique-look handles give this new dresser vintage style, but it's the dry-brushed paint treatment that offers the well-worn charm.

YOU'LL NEED:

_Bondo adhesive

_Milk paint

_Paintbrush

_Molding strips

_Miter saw

_Finish nails

_Antiquing glaze

_Clear polyurethane

_Drawer pulls

_Crafts knife

_Rag

_Drill and drill bits

1. Patch any drawer holes by filling with Bondo adhesive.

2. Prepare the milk paint by adding water to the powder (**fig. a**), following the manufacturer's instructions. Dry-brush onto the dresser to create a scratchy crosshatch effect (**fig. b**).

3. Paint molding strips white. Using a miter saw, cut and miter the molding to fit the outer edges of the drawer fronts. Attach with finish nails.

4. Apply antiquing glaze to the entire dresser. Wipe off any excess with a dry rag. When dry, coat the dresser with clear polyurethane.

5. Drill new holes for the dresser pulls and attach to the drawers.

diy tip — When using milk paint, plan to complete the project in one sitting. The paint dries quite quickly.

fig. a

fig. b

Aging Gracefully

GET THIS WEATHERED FINISH IN JUST THREE EASY STEPS.

Give your piece instant character with this easy-to-create crackle treatment. Buy all the supplies at a crafts store, and give yourself half a day to create the cottage-style seat.

YOU'LL NEED:

_Fine-grit
  sandpaper
_Tack cloth
_Paintbrush
_Primer
_Dark-color
  acrylic paint
_Crackle medium
_Light-color
  acrylic paint

1. Sand the chair, dust with a tack cloth, prime, let dry, and sand again. Paint the chair with a dark base coat. Let dry (**fig. a**).

2. Brush on the crackle medium. The thicker you paint it on, the more dramatic the crackle will be. Wait the manufacturer's recommended amount of time (about an hour) before applying the top coat of paint.

3. Brush on a light-color top coat (**fig. b**) and watch the crackle appear.

fig. a

fig. b

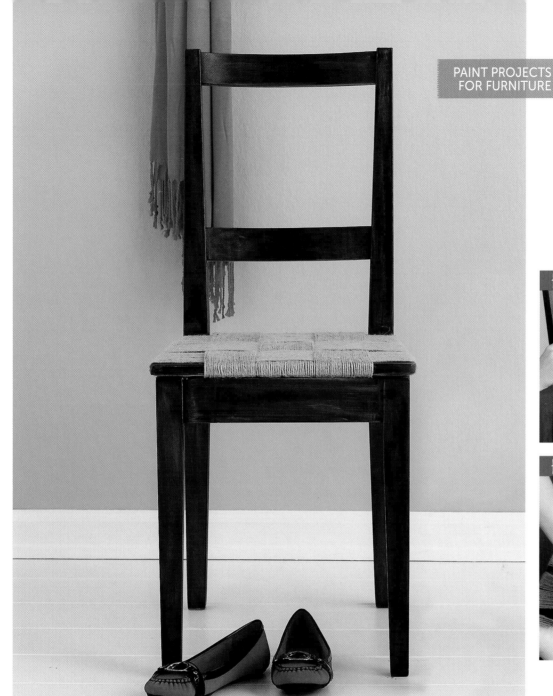

fig. a

fig. b

Redo, Take Two
GIVE THE SAME CHAIR A DIFFERENT LOOK.

If the cottage-style chair, *opposite,* isn't your cup of tea, give this clean-lined Shaker style a try. With basic garden twine, make a rush seat. Kick it up a notch with chocolate stain on the chair.

1. Remove the seat. Sand all pieces, dust with a tack cloth, and stain (**fig. a**). Let dry, following the manufacturer's directions.

2. Wrap or weave twine around the seat in the desired pattern (**fig. b**). We split the twine into three sections horizontally, then wove it over and under in three sections vertically as shown. Tie off the twine on the chair bottom when finished with each section.

3. Reattach the seat to the chair.

YOU'LL NEED:

_Fine-grit sandpaper

_Tack cloth

_Chocolate-hue
 water-base stain

_Natural-bristle brush

_Roll of garden twine

_Scissors

Chapter 3

PAINT PROJECTS FOR

walls & floors

stenciling

stamping

masking

more ideas

stenciling

This whimsical tulip on the chair back was painted as well. See the pattern on page 199.

Willowy Wallflowers

COMBINE HAND-PAINTING WITH STENCILS TO GIVE A WALL CUSTOM TREATMENT.

This fanciful blooming tree was inspired by the chair fabric and fits perfectly on a narrow wall. Start with hand-painted branches, stencil on flower and leaf motifs, then finish with hand-painted details. Position a pretty chair underneath for a delightful vignette.

YOU'LL NEED:

_Chalk

_Latex paints in desired colors

_Patterns

_Stencil plastic

_Fine-tip marker

_Self-healing cutting mat

_Crafts knife

_Stencil adhesive

_Medium-size stenciling brush

_Paper towels

_Artist's liner brush

1. Draw a tree trunk and branches on the wall using chalk, then fill in using paint and an artist's brush. Let dry. This tree is painted in sections, revealing joints in various places, and was designed specifically to grow out of the container and flow gracefully over the chair.

2. Use the patterns on page 198 and a fine-tip marker to trace the flower and leaf designs onto stencil plastic in your desired size. Lay the traced stencil plastic on a self-healing cutting mat. Use a crafts knife to cut out the design (**fig. a**). Some flowers shown are composed of different colors. Cut an overlay for each color or plan to hand-paint additional colors and details over the base flower shape when it's dry.

3. Spray the back side of a stencil with stencil adhesive. Apply the stencil to the desired place on the branch on the wall and smooth in place. Dip a medium-size stenciling brush into a small amount of paint and blot the excess paint onto a paper towel. Use a gentle circular or light tapping motion to fill in the stencil openings (**fig. b**).

4. Continue to stencil all flowers and leaves. Add final hand-painted details as desired using an artist's liner brush.

fig. a

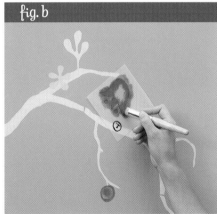
fig. b

THE PALETTE:
juicy hues

This lively color scheme is sure to grow on you. Wonderfully whimsical, these hues are undeniably ripe for the picking.

Orange plays a supportive role with tiny touches of tangerine.

Here cherry red is bold and sweet at the same time.

Sour apple green lets this scheme pucker up with a powerful punch.

A tasteful blueberry hue completes the fruit basket scheme.

Playful Paisley

THIS ALLOVER MOTIF GIVES AN ACCENT WALL GRAPHIC POP.

A bright, fresh color scheme and an oversize paisley-motif stencil give the wall in the trendy bedroom *opposite*
its graphic pop. While the pattern looks as though the stencil repeats are placed at random, a careful
examination reveals that they are actually plotted in groups of four, arranged in a pattern of diagonal rows.

YOU'LL NEED:

_Stencils

_Stencil adhesive

_Pale green latex
  paint

_Paint tray

_Stencil roller

_Paper towels

1. Spray the back of the first stencil overlay with the stencil adhesive.

2. Apply the first overlay to the wall, adhesive side down, gently patting and smoothing to ensure
that all areas have adhered well (**fig. a**).

3. Pour a small amount of pale green paint into the paint tray. Saturate the stencil roller and roll
off the excess paint onto a stack of absorbent paper towels. Too much paint on the roller can
cause the paint to bleed under the stencil. Using light pressure on the stencil roller, apply the
paint onto the stencil (**fig. b**). Check to make sure all stencil openings have been covered and
fill in where necessary. Remove the stencil and let the paint dry.

4. Spray the back side of the second overlay. Line up the registration marks of the second overlay
and press into place (**fig. c**).

5. Repeat Step 3 to stencil the overlay (**fig. d**). Let dry. Continue by placing the first overlay in the
next position and repeating Steps 2–4. Respray with adhesive after every 5 to 10 uses.

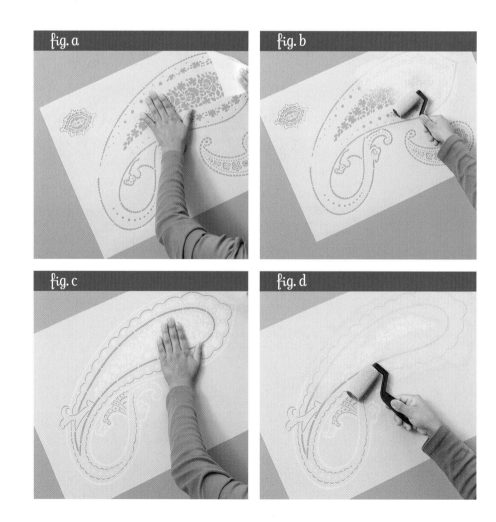

fig. a

fig. b

fig. c

fig. d

Stencil your design randomly or plan a layout as done here with groups of four paisley motifs.

Fancy This

THIS IS NOT YOUR MOTHER'S DAINTY LACE.

Who says lace can't be funky? This take on vintage-inspired frilly floral will make you want to twist and shout.

YOU'LL NEED:

_Primer

_Latex paint to suit
 your floor surface

_Paint roller and tray

_Stencil

_Stencil adhesive

_Foam roller

_Polyurethane sealer

1. Prime and paint your floor with a top coat that has a durable, glossy finish. Ask the paint pro at your local home improvement center which paint is best for your surface, be it concrete, wood, cut vinyl, or canvas floorcloth.

2. When dry, use a repositionable stencil and a foam stencil roller to apply the design. Apply stencil adhesive to the back of the stencil as often as needed to prevent paint seepage around the edges. Seal with polyurethane.

Climbing the Walls

FINE VINES GIVE THIS WALL FOCAL-POINT STATUS.

Who needs a headboard when a playful pattern this pretty is behind the bed?

YOU'LL NEED:

_Vine pattern

_Stencil plastic

_Crafts knife

_Latex paint in aqua
 and cream

_Paint roller and tray

_Tape measure

_Stencil adhesive

_Foam roller

1. Enlarge the pattern on page 200 to the desired size. Trace onto the stencil plastic and cut out.

2. Paint walls light aqua blue. Locate the center of the wall and mark near the floor. Measure and mark about every 15 inches across the wall in both directions to determine vertical placement of the stencil.

3. Spray the stencil back with stencil adhesive and position at the center marking. Use a foam stencil roller and creamy white paint to apply the leaf pattern. Reposition and reapply adhesive as needed. Let dry.

Pattern Play

LET AN ALLOVER STENCIL DRESS AN ACCENT WALL.

With quiltlike charm, this overall wall pattern makes a delightful backdrop for artwork and accessories.
A tone-on-tone palette subdues what could be a too-busy design.

YOU'LL NEED:

_Latex paint in two
   tones of green

_Paint roller and tray

_Stencil

_Stencil adhesive

_Foam roller

Paint the wall light green. Spray stencil adhesive on the back of the stencil and apply to the wall. Use a foam roller and medium green paint to apply the motif. Remove the stencil and reposition using the registration marks. Repeat, applying stencil adhesive as needed. Let dry.

diy tip If your stencil just has one impression, an allover pattern may test your patience if applying to a large area. Make one or more duplicates, so you can stencil multiple impressions at once.

Step It Up
WRAP STAIR RISERS AND TREADS IN DELIGHTFUL DESIGN.

No carpet? No problem. Visually soften wood floors and stairs with a stencil that mimics a pretty patterned carpet runner.

Determine the desired width of the pattern and cut or mask the stencil accordingly. Use stencil adhesive to secure the stencil to the first riser, wrapping around and then securing to the tread. Stencil medallions with one color and dotted lines with a second color. Carefully remove the stencil and line up using the registration marks to continue the pattern up and over the next step until done. Let dry. To protect, seal with clear polyurethane. Let dry.

YOU'LL NEED:

_Stencil

_Stencil adhesive

_Stencil brush

_Latex paint

_Polyurethane
  sealer

Going Full Circle
CREATE MODERN STYLE WITH LARGE-SCALE MOTIFS.

A mix of four sophisticated neutral shades gives this stenciled wall a designer style that mimics high-end wallpaper. But look, no seams!

YOU'LL NEED:

_Latex paint

_Paint roller and tray

_Chalk

_Measuring tape

_Multilayer stencil

_Stencil adhesive

_Foam roller

1. Paint the wall beige and let dry. Use chalk and a measuring tape to mark grid lines according to the size of your stencil. Plot where the pattern will land on the wall and determine the best starting point before stenciling.

2. Spray the "bordered" stencil with stencil adhesive and use a foam roller and tan paint to apply to the wall. Reposition and continue until done with this stencil. Let dry.

3. Spray the "dashed circle" stencil with adhesive and apply over the first stencil using cream paint and stencil registration guide marks. Apply between the first stencils using light brown paint. Let dry.

4. Apply the octagonal stencil inside half of the dashed circles (as shown) using yellow paint and registration guide marks. Let dry. Gently wipe off the chalk lines and adhesive residue.

Follow the stencil manufacturer's instructions and registration marks when applying multilayer stencils.

fig. a

YOU'LL NEED:

_Linoleum floor
  covering
_Plastic drop cloth
_Paint roller and
  extension handle
_Paint tray
_White latex primer
_Latex paint in white,
  bright yellow, and
  soft yellow
_Large and small
  zinnia stencils
_Stencil adhesive
_Foam roller
_Finish sealer

Mellow Yellow

NOTHING PICKS YOU UP LIKE FLOWERS UNDERFOOT.

Add pretty pattern to your floor with paint, eye-catching zinnia stencils, and a remnant of
linoleum from a home improvement center.

1. Unroll the linoleum floor covering onto the plastic drop cloth bottom side up and allow to
   relax until flat. Use the paint roller to apply one coat of primer. Let dry. Apply two coats of
   bright yellow paint, letting dry between coats.

2. Determine the placement of the zinnias, then spray the back of the large stencil with stencil
   adhesive and apply to the linoleum. Pour white paint into the paint tray and use a foam roller
   to apply a small amount of paint to the stencil using light pressure to fill all areas **(fig. a)**.
   Remove and reposition the stencil. Repeat until all large zinnias are painted. Let dry.

3. Repeat these steps to apply the small zinnia stencil. Let dry. Apply three coats of finish sealer,
   letting it dry between coats.

stamping

As an alternative to this random scattering of flowers, achieve a more organized pattern by stamping the flowers in staggered rows and columns.

Pretty in Pink

THESE PINK PETALS WILL TICKLE ANY GIRL'S FANCY.

Control this design with random or planned spacing of the flowers. Here, the flowers were applied
casually and approximately the same distance apart.

YOU'LL NEED:

_Latex paints in four
  shades of pink

_Paint roller and tray

_Wool pad

_Adhesive-back
  crafts foam

_Flower pattern

_Acrylic block

_Paper plate

_Foam roller

1. Base-coat the wall with light pink. Let dry. To produce the blended effect, randomly brush on
lighter pale pink and medium pink paints.

2. Working quickly and while the paint is still wet, blot and tap with a wool pad, blending to create
a subtly mottled surface. Finish one wall at a time; let dry.

3. To make the stamp, peel the backing off two sheets of adhesive-back crafts foam and layer
onto a third sheet to join the three with the backing of the third sheet intact and on the
bottom. Weight the layered foam down with books for about an hour to secure bond.

4. Print the pattern on page 200 to the desired size and trace the pattern onto the bonded foam.
Cut out the shapes, peel the adhesive backing from the foam and adhere to the block **(fig. a)**.

5. Pour a small amount of darker pink paint onto a paper plate. Using the foam roller, apply paint
to the surface of the flower stamp. Press the stamp onto the wall using firm pressure. Remove
the stamp without sliding it. Repeat, placing flowers approximately 5–8 inches apart **(fig. b)**.

fig. a

fig. b

diy tip

Mottled walls, created
with three shades of pink
and a wool pad, are kept
pale to let the flower
motif stand out. Simple,
graphic shapes work best
for homemade stamps
such as the one used for
this design.

From the Fridge
WHO KNEW VEGGIES COULD BE SO MUCH FUN?

Treat a section of wall to flower motifs created with heads of cabbage. Use a range of blues and keep things interesting by working with cabbages of various sizes.

YOU'LL NEED:

_Latex paint in light
  and medium blue

_Paint roller and tray

_Painter's tape

_Sharp knife

_Cabbages

_Foam roller

1. Paint the wall light blue. Let dry. Use painter's tape to section off a 3- to 4-foot vertical strip.

2. Use a sharp knife to cut cabbage heads in half, getting a good chop so you end up with a flat surface for better stamping.

3. Use a foam roller to apply medium blue paint to the cabbage. Firmly press the cabbage on the wall. Repeat with random placement, loading the cabbage with paint as desired and alternating with different-size cabbages (**fig. a**). For the leaf shapes, roll paint onto cabbage leaves and press on the wall. Let dry.

4. Remove the painter's tape.

diy tip

Test the stamp on a paper towel to view the impression and remove excess paint. If the cabbage "opens up" after cutting, press it on the wall and gently rotate it to get a good impression. Take a fresh cut if needed to flatten the surface.

fig. a

The natural moisture from the cabbage will add a watercolor look. For a crisper image, roll with paint after each impression.

Dot to Dot

CREATE MODERN FLAIR WITH BASIC SHAPES.

A series of dotted circles is a fun DIY project that's sure to spark a conversation.

YOU'LL NEED:

_Latex paints in two
   shades of green
   and white
_Paint roller and tray
_Glaze medium
_Soft rag
_Adhesive-back
   crafts foam
_Cardboard
_Leather punch
_Hammer
_Pattern
_Plexiglas block
_Paper plate
_Foam roller

1. For the color-washed wall, base-coat the wall light green. Let dry. Mix 4 parts glaze medium to 1 part bright green paint, making 2 cups glaze mixture for every 8 square feet of wall surface.

2. Scrunch a soft rag and dip it into the glaze mixture. Wash onto the wall using a circular motion (**fig. a**). Use a brush for corners and around the molding, then go over the surface with the rag to remove brushstrokes. Let dry. Repeat the glaze application to create a second layer.

3. To make the stamp, peel the backing off two sheets of adhesive-back crafts foam and layer them onto a third sheet to join the three with the backing of the third sheet intact and on the bottom. Set books on the layered foam for about an hour to secure the bond. Place the bonded foam on cardboard and punch out dots using a leather punch and hammer (**fig. b**).

4. Enlarge the pattern on page 200 to the desired size and place under a Plexiglas block. Peel the adhesive backing from the foam dots and adhere to the block using the pattern underneath as a guide (**fig. c**).

5. Determine the placement of the stamp, either random or staggered in horizontal lines like these. Put a small amount of white paint on a paper plate. Using a foam roller, apply paint to the surface of the stamp. Press the stamp onto the wall using firm pressure (**fig. d**). Remove the stamp without sliding it. Repeat until done. Let dry.

fig. a

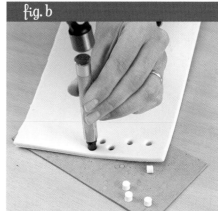

fig. b

diy tip

Because it's transparent, a Plexiglas block allows you to easily align the stamp motif where you want it before pressing it to the surface.

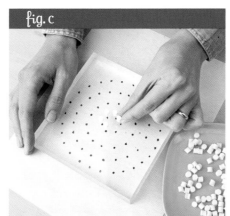

fig. c

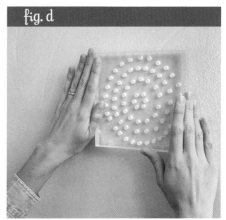

fig. d

Geometric Genius

JUST A LITTLE DAPPLE DOWN UNDER.

A scrap of sheet vinyl flipped upside down makes a perfect canvas for creativity. Grab kitchen sponges and foam stencil brushes, dip in paint, and dapple to make this graphic floorcloth.

YOU'LL NEED:

_Vinyl sheet

_Latex primer

_Latex paints

_Paint roller and tray

_Painter's tape

_Foam spouncer

_Foam stencil brush

_Sponge

_Polyurethane

1. Prime the vinyl sheet. Let dry, then roll on two coats of latex paint in the desired color, letting it dry between coats. Use semigloss paint for extra durability. Using painter's tape, mask off a border for the dot pattern and paint in the desired color. Apply dots using a foam spouncer (**fig. a**).

2. For the interior pattern, make guidelines using parallel strips of painter's tape. Use a foam stencil brush and one end of a sponge to create this graphic pattern. Dab the sponge in paint, pounce it on paper to remove excess paint, and press it on the floorcloth. Let dry.

3. Finish with two coats of clear polyurethane.

fig. a

Use What You Have

THIS THRIFTY STAMP WILL HAVE YOU RUNNING IN CIRCLES.

You'll be strapped to find a headboard more economical than this one. Just press it on using a paper towel tube. You don't even need to invest in a special stamp.

1. Paint the wall medium blue. Let dry.

2. Tape off a rectangle to the desired size for a headboard. Paint light blue. Let dry.

3. Using a paper towel tube as a stamp, dip the end of the tube in white paint and press on the top left corner of the rectangle. Moving horizontally, make another impression so the second circle slightly touches the first. Repeat along the entire length of the rectangle, then move to the second row, pressing and loading the tube as needed until done. Remove the tape. Let dry.

YOU'LL NEED:

_Latex paints in light blue, medium blue, and white

_Paint roller and tray

_Painter's tape

_Paper towel tube

masking

The larger the pattern, the less time it takes to tape off and complete a masked project like this.

Weave Your Way

WOW WALLS WITH THIS WOVEN WONDER.

Talk about attention-grabbing! This exploded cane pattern will wake any sleepyhead faster than a cup of joe.

YOU'LL NEED:

_Latex paints in pale
  and chartreuse
  greens
_Paint roller and tray
_2-inch painter's
  tape
_Artist's brush
_Acrylic matte
  medium

1. Paint the wall pale green. Let dry.

2. Using 2-inch painter's tape and **fig. a** as a guide, make the wall grid, creating 18-inch squares divided by horizontal and vertical stripes spaced 3 inches apart. For best results, add angled lines last. Use an artist's brush to apply a light coat of acrylic matte medium to the taped edges to prevent paint seepage. Let dry.

3. Paint the top coat of chartreuse green. Remove the tape as soon as the paint has set, usually about two hours.

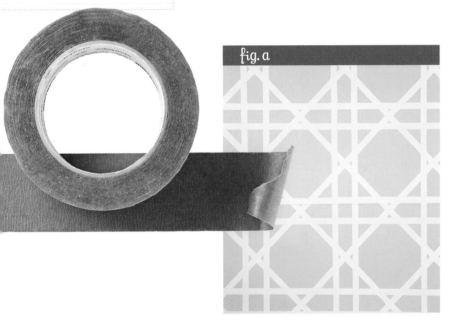

fig. a

THE PALETTE:
wake-up call

Drenched in electric hues, this room is anything but dull. This invigorating scheme is sure to perk up your day.

There's no ignoring this glowing chartreuse green.

Even when used sparingly in accents, red demands attention.

A vibrant shade of blue holds its own in this bold palette.

Calmer yet confident, Kelly green swoops in to tone things down.

Dazzling Diamonds

RESERVE THIS TIME-INTENSIVE PROJECT FOR AN ACCENT WALL.

Playful and unique, harlequin diamonds add energy to a room, especially when painted in a large scale and bold color. With all the measuring and taping, this doesn't top the quick and easy project list, but the result makes it worth the time investment.

YOU'LL NEED:

_Latex paints in light
  and lime green

_Paint roller and tray

_Level

_Straightedge

_Green colored
  pencil

_Painter's tape

_Decorator's glaze

_Small paint roller

_Upholstery tacks

_Small piece of felt

1. Paint the wall light green. Let dry. Determine the height and width of the diamond pattern by sketching it out on paper according to the dimensions of your wall to better envision the scale. The ones shown are 12 inches wide by 18 inches tall.

2. Use a level with printed measurements to find and mark all the diamond points. Connect the points using a straightedge and green colored pencil (**fig. a**). Using painter's tape outside the green lines, connect the marked points of the diamonds you plan to paint lime green. Skip around, taping off as many diamonds as you can, remembering that the tape placement doesn't allow you to paint every other diamond at the same time.

3. Roll decorator's glaze or the wall's base coat over the taped edges to seal and prevent paint seepage (**fig. b**). Use a small paint roller to paint the taped-off diamonds lime green. Let dry.

4. Continue taping off and painting the remaining diamonds (**fig. c**). Remove all tape. Let dry.

5. Place a small piece of felt over upholstery tacks and use a hammer to tap them in at each diamond point (**fig. d**).

fig. a

fig. b

fig. c

fig. d

Around the Block

WITH THIS PLAYGROUND OF COLOR, YOU CAN'T HELP BUT SMILE.

Painting these bold blocks is a balance of work and play—you'll need time and patience to complete it, but the result is a fun-and-games style you'll love.

YOU'LL NEED:

_Tape measure

_Graph paper

_Paint chips

_Latex paints

_Paint roller and tray

_Colored pencil

_Level

_Painter's tape

_Chip brush

_Small paint roller

1. Measure the total height and width of each wall in inches. Sketch a scaled drawing on graph paper to determine the size and placement of blocks. The blocks shown here are 24 inches square. To visualize color, cut paint chips to fit your grid and arrange until you're pleased with the color sequence.

2. Paint the walls white. Let dry. Use a tape measure and colored pencil to measure and mark the placement of each block, then use a long level and colored pencil to connect the marks and complete the block pattern.

3. Tape off alternating blocks with the low-tack painter's tape. To seal the tape and help prevent the paint from bleeding underneath, use a chip brush to repaint the base-coat color along the taped edges of the block (**fig. a**). Let dry.

4. Use a small roller to paint each taped block (**fig. b**). Paint two coats if necessary, letting dry between coats. When the paint loses its shiny, wet look and begins to dry, carefully remove the tape. Let the paint dry.

5. Repeat the taping and painting process on adjacent blocks until the entire grid of blocks is complete (**fig. c**). Remove all tape. Let dry.

fig. a

fig. b

fig. c

THE PALETTE:
pure stimulation

Hot and cool hues create bands of saturated color. No room for pale or pastel in this stimulating mix—the bolder the better in this invigorating color adventure.

Passionate purple is a perfect segue between red and blue.

Firecracker red pops off the wall and onto key accessories.

Deep tones of royal blue anchor this scheme.

Don't hesitate to throw magenta into this fanciful mix of hues.

Perfecting Plaid

THIS CHARMING FLOOR WILL LEAVE YOU ANYTHING BUT BLUE.

To brighten your porch floor, paint an oversize plaid pattern on the board planks using white and two shades of all-American blue.

YOU'LL NEED:

_Paper

_Pencil

_Exterior primer

_Paint roller and tray

_Exterior deck paint
  in white, light blue,
  and medium blue

_Painter's tape

1. Map out your pattern on a piece of paper to determine the block size. Prime the floor. Let dry. Use a roller to paint it with white exterior deck paint. Let dry.

2. Mark off squares using a pencil. Mask off and paint the appropriate squares using light blue paint. Let dry. Mask and paint the medium blue squares. Always mask to the outside of the pattern lines, and allow all paint to dry thoroughly between applications.

For a durable, lasting finish, look for good-quality floor paint with polyurethane mixed in the paint.

Walk This Way

STEP UP AND TRY THIS FUN RUNNER.

Though it's a bit more work to lay out a plaid pattern on stairs than on a flat floor, the result is well worth the effort.

Prime the stairs, then paint them with two coats of crisp white floor paint. Once you determine the placement of the squares, paint the design following the instructions for the porch plaid on the opposite page. After the blue paints are thoroughly dry, tape off and paint a green border. Let dry. Top with a few coats of polyurethane (unless it's in your floor paint already), letting dry between coats.

YOU'LL NEED:

_Latex primer

_Paint roller and tray

_Floor paints in white, two shades of blue, and green

_Painter's tape

_Polyurethane

The top coat color (which is mixed with the glaze) will appear more dominant in the pattern.

Go with the Grain

ONE LITTLE TOOL, ONE BIG IMPACT.

This tone-on-tone technique is sure to grow on you. Go modern with this nature-inspired pattern by using colors like this blue or even sunshiny yellow or raspberry red. The wood-grain tool comes in different widths, so you can get the look of wide or narrow planks. Or go crazy and try alternating the tool for varying plank widths.

YOU'LL NEED:

_Painter's tape

_Latex paint in two
  shades of blue

_Paint roller and tray

_Glaze medium

_Plastic container

_Wood-grain tool

1. Mask the baseboard and chair rail with painter's tape. Paint the wall the lighter blue color.

2. In a plastic container, mix 4 parts glaze medium with 1 part medium blue paint. Working quickly and in 3-foot sections, roll the glaze mixture on the wall.

3. Starting at the top of the wall, pull the wood-graining tool down the wall to create a plank, rocking up and down as you go. For the next plank, slightly overlap the first (**fig. a**).

4. Wipe excess glaze off the tool as needed and continue until the wall is complete. Remove the tape and let dry.

diy tip
Glaze extends the working time to about an hour, so if you're not happy with the results, just brush on more glaze and start over.

fig. a

THE PALETTE:
true blue

Who needs a rainbow of colors when just a few will do? This country palette shows that sometimes less is more.

Don't forget that wood finishes add rich color, too.

It takes two hues of blue to pull off this tone-on-tone texture.

Choose an easy-to-love hue like sky blue as the key player.

Warm antique or off-white colors aren't as cold or stark as pure white.

Strictly Ornamental

TRY THIS DELICATE DOT-TO-DOT PATTERN.

At first glance, this pattern looks complicated, but it's just a combination of C and S shapes, dots, lines, and elongated triangles.

YOU'LL NEED:

_Latex paints

_Paint roller and tray

_Flexible measuring
 tape

_Level

_Chalk

_Paper plate

_Artist's brushes

_Pattern

1. Paint the wall the desired color. Measure the height of the wall in inches and divide by 12 to determine the number of horizontal repeats. Use a level and chalk to mark horizontal lines at 12-inch intervals (**fig. a**).

2. Attach a measuring tape to the wall above one chalk line. Pour a small amount of paint onto a paper plate and dip the end of an artist's brush handle into the paint. Make one dot every 12 inches along the chalk lines, moving the tape as needed until all lines are dotted (**fig. b**).

3. Using the pattern on page 201 as a guide, make vertical rows of dots at each 12-inch interval along the horizontal rows of dots. Begin filling in the scroll designs on either side of each vertical row of dots (**fig. c**).

4. Continue to fill in details, painting lines and making dots in repetitive groupings until the desired effect is achieved (**fig. d**).

fig. a

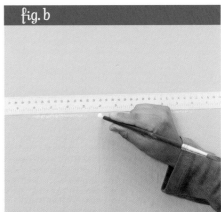

fig. b

fig. c

fig. d

When painting the scroll shapes, start and finish each with a subtle dot.

Go with Gingham

SOFTEN A SMALL SPACE WITH THIS CASUAL PATTERN.

This cheerful check is a cottage-style staple, but use the pattern sparingly on walls, as large doses can easily overwhelm the eye. You'll almost always want to pair the check color with white, as two colors would be visually chaotic unless a subtle tone-on-tone palette is the look you desire.

YOU'LL NEED:

_Latex satin paint in
  white and lavender
_Paint roller and tray
_Plastic container
_Glaze medium
_Notched squeegee
_Lint-free cloth

---

1. Paint the lavender base color. Let dry.

2. In a plastic container, mix 4 parts glaze medium with 1 part white paint, then roll on the wall. Working in 3-foot masked-off sections, pull the notched squeegee down the wall, making vertical stripes. Wipe excess glaze off the squeegee with a damp lint-free cloth. Repeat across the section, working quickly so the glaze doesn't dry (**fig. a**).

3. Starting at the top of the wall, drag the tool across the previously combed area to create horizontal stripes (**fig. b**). Repeat down the section. Let the glaze dry and remove the tape.

diy tip

A steady hand will produce crisp, straight checks, but try a slight waver to make the pattern more casual and flowing.

fig. a

fig. b

THE PALETTE:
sweet as can be

If you're looking for cottage charm, this is the palette for you. Gentle and airy, these delightful hues are like a breath of fresh air.

Lovable lavender is a nice alternative to typical cottage blue.

Pink hues—both punchy and pale—are icing on the cake.

Grass green brings a little nature to the sweet scheme.

Crisp and clean, white holds the breezy mix together.

Wonderfully Worn

DENIM STYLE SHOUTS KICKED-BACK COMFORT.

Looking for that perfect fit? Slip into pure comfort by dressing your walls in denim. This texture is a snap with the right tools and can work with any color, so think beyond blue!

1. Paint the walls with semigloss blue paint. Let dry. In a plastic container, mix 4 parts glaze medium to 1 part blue paint.

2. Working quickly and in masked-off 3-foot sections, roll a thin layer of the mixture on the wall. Starting at the top left corner of the section, drag the dry denim weaver brush across the section from left to right in a smooth, firm stroke (**fig. a**). Wipe the brush with a damp lint-free cloth. Directly on top of the first stroke, drag across the section from right to left using the opposite side of the brush. Wipe the brush again. On top of the first strokes, repeat the left-to-right then right-to-left strokes a second time. Continue down the length of the wall.

3. For the vertical strokes, start at the top and sweep down to the floor, lightly skimming the surface to leave vertical lines but not erase the horizontal lines (**fig. b**). Wipe the brush and continue until the vertical lines are complete.

4. Roll the check roller in horizontal and vertical passes across the entire section (**fig. c and fig. d**). Remove the painter's tape from the first section and move onto the next. Let dry.

diy tip

If the check roller texture is disappearing, wait about one minute and roll again. Sometimes the glaze is too wet to hold the added texture.

fig. a

fig. b

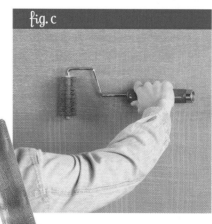

fig. c

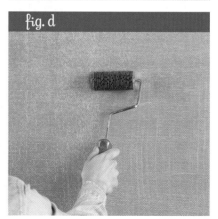

fig. d

If you don't want to tackle an entire wall, or if you rent and can't paint the walls, create an accent panel like this.

The bigger the squares, the more modern the look, but avoid squares larger than 24 inches unless your room is massive.

Checkmate

PRACTICE MAKES PERFECT WITH THIS PRETTY PATTERN.

A wood-grain pattern takes this checkerboard floor to a whole new level. Although it looks tricky, it's easy to master with practice and patience. Perfect your technique on a sample board first.

YOU'LL NEED:

_Palm sander

_Trisodium phosphate solution

_Fine-grade sandpaper

_Tack cloth

_Floor paint in white and ebony

_Paint roller and tray

_Laser pointer level

_Painter's tape

_Glaze

_Paintbrush

_Wood-grain tool

_Epoxy sealant

1. Prep the floor by sanding off any old varnish and washing with a trisodium phosphate (TSP) solution. Buff with a fine-grade sandpaper and wipe down with a tack cloth. Paint the floor white. Let dry. Determine the desired square size; these are 12 inches. Starting in the center of the room and working outward, use a laser pointer level to connect your marks, making a diamond pattern; pencil in lines.

2. Mask off alternating squares using painter's tape. Mix ebony paint with glaze in a 1:1 ratio. Brush the glaze mix onto the square (**fig. a**).

3. Drag a wood-graining tool through the square (**fig. b**). Lift off the tape before the paint dries completely. Repeat in all masked squares. Let dry. Mask the remaining squares and repeat the glaze and wood-grain process.

4. For a super-hard finish, apply 2 or 3 coats of epoxy sealant that doesn't yellow, letting dry between coats.

diy tip This ebony and white color combination has a modern, earthy feel. Experiment on plywood with different color schemes.

fig. a

fig. b

Steady Stripes

FREEHAND MAKES A QUICK JOB OF THIS TECHNIQUE.

With these laid-back lines, there's no need to bother with tape.

YOU'LL NEED:

_Latex paint in blue
  and green

_Paint roller and tray

_Green colored pencil

_Level

_Trim brush

1. Base-coat the wall with blue paint. Determine stripe width and divide the wall into even increments. Using a level and green colored pencil, draw vertical lines up the wall (**fig. a**).

2. Using a trim brush, green paint, and a steady hand, cut in both sides of the stripe, using long vertical strokes and covering the pencil line (**fig. b**). Fill in the center of the stripe. Repeat for all stripes. Let dry.

fig. a

fig. b

If you don't want to tackle an entire wall, or if you rent and can't paint the walls, create an accent panel like this.

YOU'LL NEED:

_Latex semigloss
 paint in aqua blue
_Paint roller and tray
_Metallic silk paint
_Glaze medium
_Plastic container
_Painter's tape
_Wallpaper paste
 brush
_Lint-free cloth

Smooth as Silk

A FANCY FINISH INSPIRED BY FABRIC.

Dress your wall with a lustrous faux silk surface that's both easy and pleasing. A metallic pearlescent paint is the secret to this elegant treatment you'll be tempted to touch.

1. Paint the wall with aqua blue semigloss paint. Let dry.

2. In a plastic container, mix 1 part metallic silk paint and 1 part glaze medium. Working in masked-off 3-foot sections, roll the mixture onto the wall, smoothing out by rolling vertically until the mixture is coated evenly.

3. Drag a dry wallpaper paste brush through the glaze from top to bottom in one continuous motion, creating a vertical pattern in the wet glaze. Wipe excess glaze off the brush with a lint-free cloth as needed. Remove the tape and repeat in all sections until complete. Let dry.

Chapter 4

PAINT PROJECTS FOR

artwork &
accessories

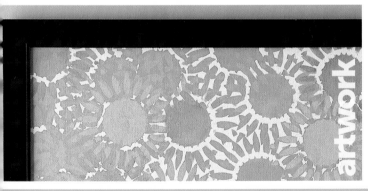

artwork

accessories

PAGES 112–123

PAGES 124–137

If you can't find a bedsheet the right color, dye one using fabrics dye.

Wall Flowers

A PAINTED SHEET MAKES SHOWY ART.

Don't consider yourself an artist? No sweat! Just stamp tons of small flowers in a mix of colors until they grow into enormous blossoms. Then, secure the green-dyed twin sheet to a homemade wood frame like an artist's stretched canvas. Mask ceiling, baseboards, and trim with painter's tape. Paint the entire wall in the light olive green base-coat color. Paint two coats if necessary. Leave the tape on and let the paint dry overnight.

YOU'LL NEED:

_Marker

_Flower pattern

_Sticky-back foam

_Scissors

_Wood blocks

_Paintbrush

_Acrylic paints

_Twin bedsheet

1. Using a permanent marker and the pattern from page 202, trace the flower shape onto self-adhesive crafts foam (you'll want a different foam flower for each color of flower you want to merge into the big blossom) (**fig. a**). The flower stems and leaves are easy to freehand with a paintbrush once you're done stamping.

2. Cut out the foam flower shapes (don't forget the hole in the middle). Peel off the foam's backing paper and stick each shape to a block of wood to create a stamp (**fig. b**).

3. Use a paintbrush to dab paint onto the stamp (**fig. c**). Lay the paint on thick in some areas of the stamp and barely at all in others to create texture and dimension—a chic Italian impasto look!

4. Tape a twin bedsheet to a protected work surface and stamp one flower at a time, overlapping to create each large blossom (**fig. d**). Repeat with the other flower colors, letting dry between colors. Hand-paint stems and then leaves. Let dry.

diy tip
The trick to stretching a sheet taut and square is in the order you attach the sides: Staple the top edge to the top of the frame first, always working from the middle out. Stretch it to the bottom of the frame next, then do the sides last.

fig. a

fig. b

fig. c

fig. d

This Calls for Seconds

TRY THESE BUTTERFLY SILHOUETTES AS SHAPELY ARTWORK.

With just a few minutes and a few materials, you'll create an art project so easy you can't stop at just one! Choose from nature silhouettes, people, pets—even shapely furnishings are fun to profile.

YOU'LL NEED:

_Butterfly patterns

_Sticker or vinyl inkjet paper

_Scissors

_Paper punch

_Plate

_Spray paint

_Crafts knife

_Picture hanger

_Adhesive spray

1. Using the patterns on page 202, copy the motifs onto sticker or vinyl paper. Cut out with scissors. Use a paper punch for tiny details (**fig. a**).

2. Secure the motif to a plate, making sure the edges are sealed down (**fig. b**). Shake the spray can well and follow the manufacturer's instructions to spray-paint the plate (**fig. c**). Apply several coats if needed, letting the paint dry between coats.

3. Remove the motif and let the paint dry (**fig. d**). Touch up the rough edges using a crafts knife. Use permanent adhesive to secure a picture hanger to the back of the plate.

fig. a

fig. b

fig. c

fig. d

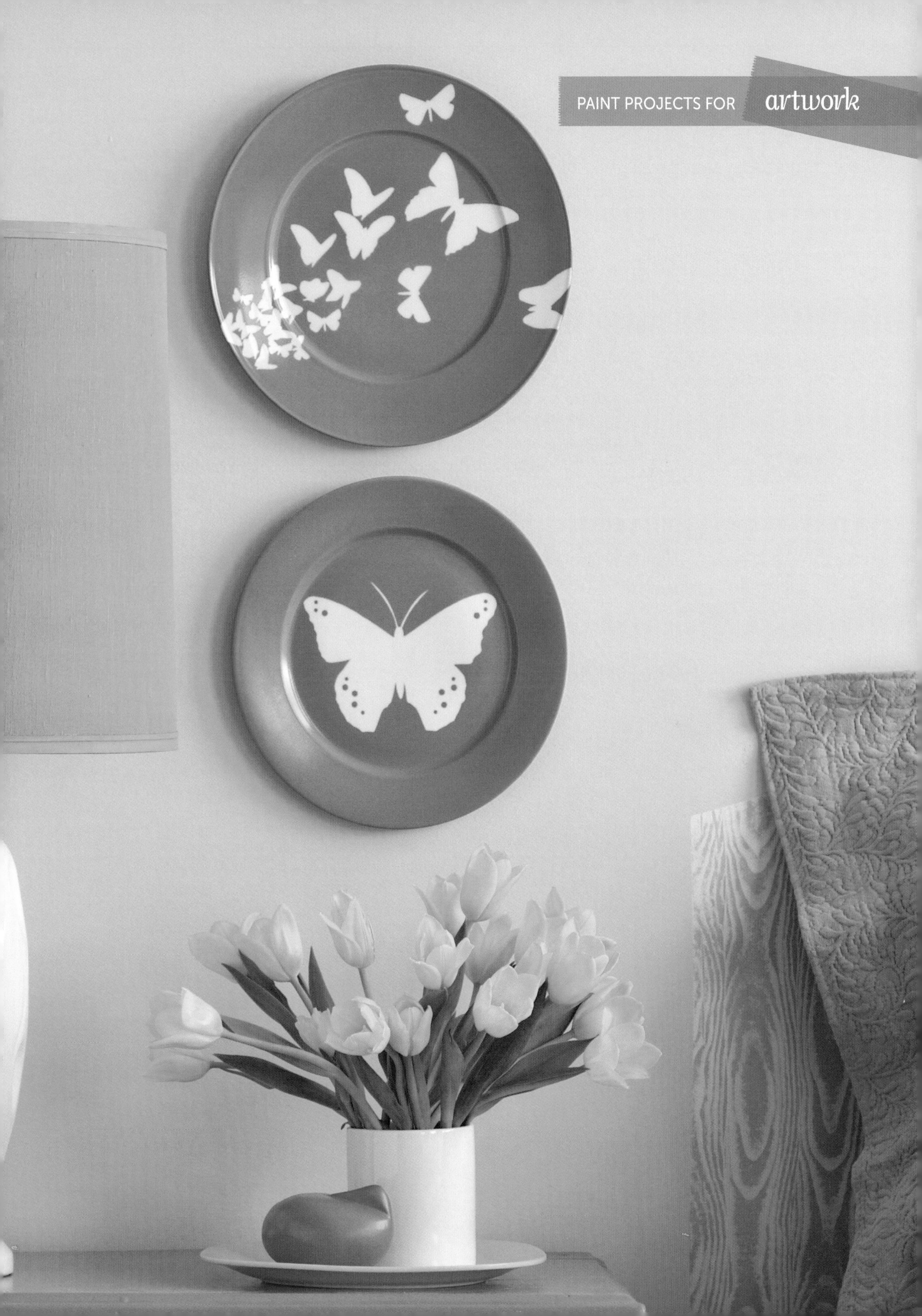

Something to Chirp About

LET THIS LUCKY CRICKET LOOSE IN YOUR ROOM.

If the other screen-printed projects in this book haven't already tempted you to try this paint technique, you simply can't pass by this little guy.

YOU'LL NEED:

_Spray stain

_Birch plywood

_Picture wire

_Clear transparency film

_Emulsion

_Clear tape

_Screen-printing screen

_Screen-printing ink or acrylic paint

_Squeegee

1. Use spray stain to finish a piece of birch plywood. Let dry, then secure picture wire to the back.

2. Choose a motif and copy onto clear transparency film in black and white and on the darkest setting.

3. In a room with only a red light, coat both sides of the screen with a thin layer of emulsion and let it dry in a dark room.

4. Tape the transparency to the screen, then expose the screen to bright light for an hour.

5. Remove the transparency and wash the screen under running water to remove the emulsion where the image was (**fig. a**). Let dry.

6. Position the screen over the plywood and place a line of screen-printing ink or acrylic paint on the screen above the image. Use a squeegee to pull the paint down over the image, making a couple of passes until the area is covered. Carefully remove the screen and let the paint dry.

fig. a

diy tip If you're not up for stretching your own canvas, you can use a prestretched one from an art or crafts store. Or skip the canvas altogether and stencil on a mat board or heavy stock paper.

YOU'LL NEED:

_Stencil

_Canvas

_Stencil brush

_Acrylic paints

_Stretcher bars

_Frame

Cheap and Chic

MAKE ROOM FOR LAYERED BLOOMS.

Eye-catching art doesn't have to drain your bank account. Use repetitive sunflower shapes to create original works that both your artsy and thrifty sides will love.

1. To make this stunning artwork, start with a sunflower stencil and raw canvas. Randomly stencil the design using a stencil brush and three shades of orange, letting the paint dry between colors.

2. Stretch the canvas on stretcher bars and hang it in the frame.

Psychedelic Frame

FOR THIS TIE-DYE EFFECT, JUST PLAY WITH SPRAY.

It's not often you get the go-ahead to decorate graffiti-style, so don't miss this far-out photo frame facelift.

YOU'LL NEED:

_Frame

_Box

_Spray paints

1. Getting this layered look is pretty effortless. Working in a well-ventilated room, remove the glass and mat from the frame and place it in a cardboard box to protect your work area (**fig. a**).

2. Using a sweeping motion, spray the first color of paint on the frame. When dry, add the next color and so forth. Many paints dry to the touch in less than 10 minutes, so adding layers of color is quick.

fig. a

diy tip
When stamping, keep a large wet sponge in a tray nearby for quick cleanup.

Leaf a Good Impression
FILL YOUR WALL WITH A LINE OF LEAVES.

Leaves, flowers, and other objects from nature make magnificent motifs for art.

Paint small canvases with several complementary colors and let dry. Pour a small amount of paint onto a paper plate and press a large leaf picked from the great outdoors into the paint. Stamp the leaf in the center of each canvas. Let dry.

YOU'LL NEED:

_Canvases

_Acrylic paints

_Paper plate

_Leaf

Silhouette Style

TURN EVERYDAY OBJECTS INTO POP ART.

Scour your office, garage, or the hardware store for inexpensive objects sporting art-worthy shapes
(choose items you don't mind being painted).

YOU'LL NEED:

_Paperboard

_Cardboard box

_Objects

_Spray paint

1. To protect your work surface, place the paperboard inside a cardboard box.

2. Arrange your objects on the board. Spray-paint over the board and objects until well coated. Let dry, then remove the objects.

diy tip Heavier objects work well, but lighter-weight ones can be tacked down using adhesive spray.

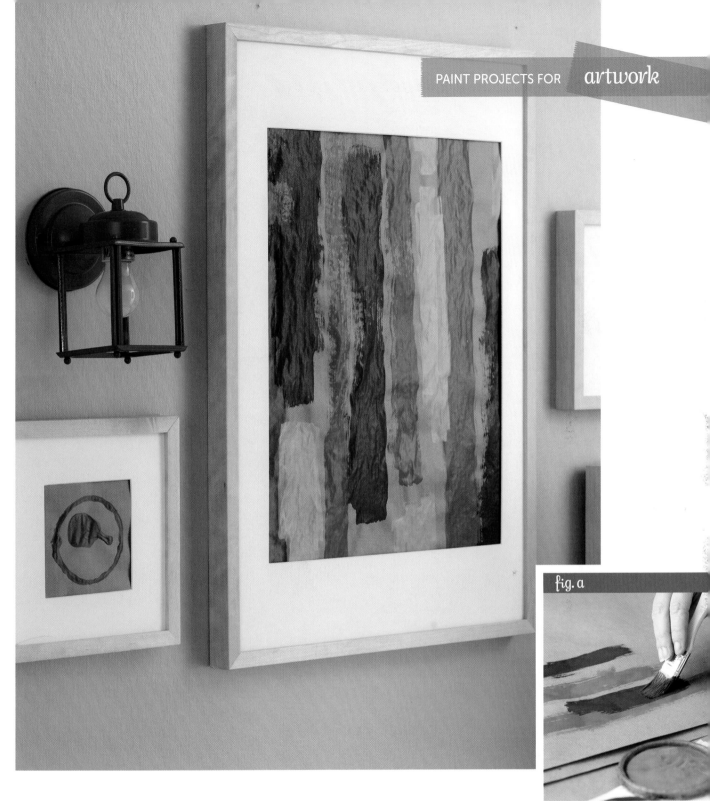

fig. a

Art in Minutes
LET THESE EASY-DO IDEAS INSPIRE YOU.

If you're short on time and money, this project is for you.

Use acrylic paints and small paintbrushes to line kraft paper with different color stripes (**fig. a**). For the abstract circle print, just paint the rim of a cup and press onto kraft paper, then dab a bit of paint inside the circle impression. Insert the kraft paper into matted frames and hang.

YOU'LL NEED:

_Acrylic paints

_Paintbrushes

_Kraft paper

_Cup

_Frames

Tableware Transformations

DON'T LET DATED DISHWARE STAND IN ART'S WAY.

Upcycle old wooden plates and platters into an enchanting wall display.

YOU'LL NEED:

_Painter's tape

_Contact paper

_Wooden plates

_Cardboard box

_Spray paints

_Pencil

_Drill

_Yarn

1. Use painter's tape and self-adhesive contact paper to mask areas of the sections of the plates you don't want painted, such as the dots, rim, and tree branch on these plates.

2. Place in a cardboard box and spray-paint over the plates until well coated, letting dry between coats if needed. Remove masking and let dry.

3. To add yarn embellishments, draw the desired design in pencil, then use a drill to make holes along the lines of the design. Thread yarn through the holes, using decorative stitches and knots.

As an alternative to yarn, try using thin ribbons or colored twine.

Try using different colors of paint for the letters and symbols. Before adding fabric to the hoops, paint them as well.

YOU'LL NEED:

_Scrapbook or crafts
 letters
_White fabric
_Pencil
_Paintbrush
_Fabrics paint
_Embroidery hoops
_Scissors

What's Your Type?

MAKE A STATEMENT WITH THIS EASY-DO ART.

Typography artwork is fabulous, but it can do a number on your pocketbook. Put this budget-friendly spin on the trend.

Arrange scrapbook or crafts letters on white fabric or canvas. Trace with a pencil, then fill in the shapes using a paintbrush and fabrics paint. When dry, stretch the fabric through an embroidery hoop and secure. Cut off extra fabric along the edges and hang.

Freshen a thrift
store lamp base
with paint. See
chapter 5 for tips
on how to paint
ceramic surfaces.

Shed Some Light

A LITTLE PAINT SHAPES UP THIS SHADE.

It's no secret that this thrift store drum shade needed a major lift. With a just a little paint,
it flaunts decorator style in no time.

YOU'LL NEED:

_Lampshade

_Cardboard box

_Green spray paint

_Painter's tape

_Paintbrush

_Dark and light
green crafts paint

_Leaft patterns

_Self-adhesive crafts
foam

_Scissors

_Plexiglas blocks

1. Place the shade in a cardboard box to protect your work surface while painting. Using several light coats, spray-paint the lampshade green until it's completely covered. Let dry.

2. Use painter's tape to mask off a line on the lampshade. Fill in using dark green crafts paint to create a stem (**fig. a**). Let dry.

3. Using the patterns on page 203, draw a small leaf shape and a larger leaf outline shape onto self-adhesive crafts foam. Cut out the foam shapes, peel off the foam's backing paper, and stick each shape to a Plexiglas block to create two stamps.

4. Pour a small amount of light green crafts paint in a dish. Press the small leaf stamp into the paint and then onto the lampshade in various places along the stem (**fig. b**). Repeat as desired with the leaf outline stamp. Let dry.

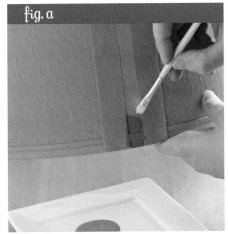
fig. a

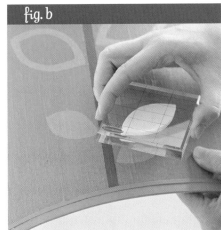
fig. b

THE PALETTE:
fruit smoothie

With fabulously fruity hues, this colorful mix is sure to quench your thirst. Perfect for a bedroom or kitchen, let this refreshing blend brighten your day.

A juicy shade of kiwi green is ripe for this scheme.

Punchy pink raspberry adds sassy sweetness.

Peel out with banana yellow as a smooth canvas for this mix.

Touches of fresh white keep these vibrant hues in check.

Printer's Block

CARVE YOUR WAY TO AN ORIGINAL DESIGN.

Get steamed up and ready to go with this stamping project. The linoleum blocks are reusable, so you can repeat your motifs again and again. And to make things even simpler, purchase a block print starter kit and you're ready to go.

YOU'LL NEED:

_Pencil

_Transfer paper

_Chisel

_Linoleum block

_Rubber ink roller

_Ink or paint

_Pencil

_Paint tray

1. Use a pencil and transfer paper to transfer your design to the linoleum block. For this teapot motif, see the pattern on page 203.

2. Using a wood chisel, carve away all the areas of the linoleum block you don't want to print. Chisels come in different sizes to make quick work of large areas and to carefully shape fine details (**fig. a**). To get the wood-print effect (the random lines that show around our design), don't chip off every surface. Once you try the stamp, you can always cut more away.

3. Use a rubber ink roller to roll ink or paint evenly onto the raised parts of the stamp block (**fig. b**). You'll get only one print per application of paint; try to reload with about the same amount of paint each time you print. Press the block onto your chosen surface. Let dry.

diy tip

If you love the shading effect shown here, leave some areas of the block uncut. For a more artful look, use uneven pressure when applying the stamp.

fig. a

fig. b

PAINT PROJECTS FOR *accessories*

Think Outside the Box
ADD DAPPER PINSTRIPES TO DULL BOXES.

Who knew combs weren't just for hair? With a special flexible combing tool, this paint technique gives plain-Jane crafts boxes top shelf status (**fig. a**).

YOU'LL NEED:

_Wooden boxes

_Latex paints

_Paintbrush

_Small container

_Glaze medium

_Flexible combing
  tool

1. Paint the wooden boxes the desired colors (for a tone-on-tone scheme, use the lighter hue as the base coat). Let dry.

2. In a small container, mix 2 parts glaze to 1 part paint. Apply a thick coat of the glaze mixture to one side of each box, then drag a combing tool across the box to remove the glaze mixture (**fig. b**). Repeat on the entire box. Let dry.

diy tip

Stray from the straight and narrow a bit by using the combing tool to create a wavy design or by applying a horizontal stripe on the box lid and a vertical stripe on the base.

fig. a

fig. b

THE PALETTE:
fun and flavorful

Cook up a new color scheme by tossing in colors of the same tone or intensity. Here yellow and mint hues are a tasty team. Though a surprise to the mix, royal blue adds a punch of needed flavor.

Warmth from mustard hues makes this scheme shine.

Butter yellow cuts the mustard by showing a softer side.

An unexpected spearmint hue cools down the tasty mix.

Berry blue enlivens the palette when spattered.

Do It Yourself *artwork & accessories* **129**

Photo Opportunity

PLUCK A FEW LEAVES FOR PATTERN INSPIRATION.

Any plain white surface, such as a picture framing mat, is fair game for a pretty perk-up.

YOU'LL NEED:

_Leaf

_Paper

_Foam spouncer

_Crafts paint

_Picture frame mat

_Paint roller

1. For the most detailed images, choose a leaf with pronounced veining (**fig. a**) and place vein side up on a piece of paper. Using a foam spouncer, dab the leaf with crafts paint until evenly coated (**fig. b**).

2. Flip the leaf over and place on the picture mat. Cover the leaf with a piece of paper to avoid getting paint on the roller, then roll over the leaf using even pressure. Remove the paper and peel off the leaf. Repeat as desired.

fig. a

fig. b

YOU'LL NEED:

_Stencil

_Stencil adhesive

_Lampshade

_Stencil brush

_Fabrics or crafts
  paints

Made in the Shade

USING SEVERAL HUES PUTS A SPIN ON THIS STENCIL.

With its shapely spa blue base and multihue zinnia shade, this lamp is a perfect bedside companion.

Spray the stencil back with stencil adhesive and position on the lampshade. Use a stencil brush to apply paint to the stencil until the exposed areas are covered. Carefully remove the stencil and wash the paint off with warm soapy water. Repeat the process with the next paint color and continue until finished. Let dry.

Bin Booster

BATH STORAGE NEVER LOOKED SO GOOD.

Treat bland canvas bins to playful color and pattern. Can you believe these dollar-store bins were originally beige?

1. For the dotted pattern, paint the bin two coats of pink, letting the paint dry between coats. Cut a 1½-inch circle from the stencil plastic. Spray the stencil back with stencil adhesive and position on the bin. Stencil the circle in orange. Remove, reposition, and repeat to complete the polka-dot pattern. Apply 2 or 3 coats of finish sealer, letting dry between coats.

2. For the stripe pattern, paint the bins two coats of coral, letting dry between coats. Use a ruler to mark off stripes of varying widths, and use painter's tape to mask every other stripe. Paint stripes the desired colors. Remove the tape and let dry. Tape off the remaining stripes adjacent to the ones already painted and paint the desired colors. Remove the tape and let dry. Spray the flower stencil back with stencil adhesive and position over the stripe pattern. Paint the stencil using a contrasting color. Remove the stencil and let dry. Apply 2 or 3 coats of finish sealer, letting dry between coats.

use photo-editing software to give any image a pixelated effect right from your computer.

fig. a

Pixel Love

PROUDLY REVEAL YOUR GEEK SIDE.

Before high-def, pixel icons reigned on computer screens. This project takes them from the screens of yesterday to the hot home decor of today.

YOU'LL NEED:

_Lampshade

_Painter's tape

_Pouncer brush

_Acrylic paints

_Pixel image

_Contact paper

1. Create diagonal stripes on a lampshade with painter's tape. Use a pouncer brush to dab acrylic paint onto the shade, creating stripes. Let dry, then remove the tape (**fig. a**).

2. Search for "pixel icons" online to find an image or use the heart pattern on page 203. Transfer the image to contact paper and cut out to create a stencil. Peel the backing from the paper and affix it to the shade. Paint the stencil over the stripes using the pouncer. Peel the stencil off and let the shade dry. Use black paint to outline the image.

Pick a Card

SMALL DESIGNS CAN LEAVE A MIGHTY MARK.

Why drop dough on expensive greeting cards when you can make your own for next to nothing and in less time than it takes to run out for one?

YOU'LL NEED:

_Cards or colored paper

_Small stencil

_Acrylic paint

_Foam spouncer

Use blank cards or fold colored paper to make your own. Place a piece of paper inside the card in case the paint bleeds through. Position a petite stencil on the front of the card and paint it with acrylic paint and a foam spouncer (**fig. a**). Remove the stencil and let dry.

fig. a

fig. a

YOU'LL NEED:

_Painter's tape

_Terra-cotta pots

_Exterior spray
 paints

_Flower pot
 hangers

On the Fence

GIVE BASIC TERRA-COTTA NEW HUES.

Revive an old fence with a grid of pretty flower pots filled with blooming annuals.

Use painter's tape to mask off the pots' rims. On a protected work surface, coat the pots with various colors of exterior spray paint (**fig. a**). Remove the tape and let dry. Suspend the pots from flower pot hangers, then fill with potting soil and pretty plants.

Favorite Ferns

A SIMPLE STENCIL LETS A PLAIN LAMP BASE SHINE.

Let fresh fronds frolic on a lamp base. This base was actually a plain green vase converted into a lamp using a lamp kit from a crafts store.

YOU'LL NEED:

_Stencil adhesive

_Stencil

_Lamp base

_Stencil brush

_Glass paint

1. Spray stencil adhesive on the back of a fern stencil and position on a flat area of the lamp base.

2. Use a stencil brush and glass paint to paint the stencil. For best results, use a small amount of paint and a pouncing motion with the brush. Remove the stencil and let dry.

E Is for Exquisite
SERVE UP STYLE WITH THIS MONOGRAM ACCENT.

Olive branch garland and an Edwardian script E turn an ordinary white serving tray into a tabletop treasure.

YOU'LL NEED:

_Stencil adhesive

_Stencils

_Tray

_Stencil brush

_Acrylic paints

1. Use stencil adhesive to secure a letter stencil in the center of the tray. Stencil using a stencil brush and the desired acrylic paint color. Remove the stencil and let dry.

2. Use stencil adhesive to secure the garland stencil around the letter and stencil in the desired colors, blending hues if desired and using different colors for the berries and leaves. Remove the stencil and let dry.

PAINT PROJECTS FOR

ceramics, glass & metal

ceramics

glass

metal

PAGES 140–145   PAGES 146–153   PAGES 154–161

fig. a

Sharpie

To really let your design shine, leave part of the lamp base bare.

Delicate Doodles

NO PATTERN HERE: JUST TRY FREESTYLE.

Brighten a basic colored lamp base with whimsical lines. A fine white oil paint marker is the perfect tool to put your sketches in the spotlight.

Using an oil paint marker, draw simple spirals and interlocking paisley or flower patterns for an intricate look **(fig. a)**. Start at the top and work your way down for best results.

YOU'LL NEED:

_Oil paint marker

_Ceramic lamp base

fig. a

Office Space
PLAYFUL CATCHALLS MAKE WORK MORE FUN.

Assign a collection of plain servingware new tasks as stylish spots to stash office supplies.

To embellish plain white dishes, use porcelain paint pens to repeat a simple circle chain pattern as desired **(fig. a)**. This cohesive, modern design and color scheme unify the eclectic mix of thrift shop pieces into efficient office organizers. If desired, bake the pieces according to the paint manufacturer's instructions to set the paint.

Let's Face It

GUESTS WILL FALL FOR THESE PAINTED LADIES.

Everyone will feel like the guest of honor when each place is set with a personalized painted plate.

Using a photo as a starting point, draw the shape and fine features using a porcelain paint pen. A paintbrush is better for adding a little blush or a head of hair. Keep acetone (nail polish remover works well) and tissues on hand to remove any mistakes. Bake the pieces according to the paint manufacturer's instructions to set the paint.

YOU'LL NEED:

_Porcelain paint pen
 and paints
_Paintbrush
_Porcelain dishware
_Acetone
_Tissues
_Oven

diy tip
Although they should be food-safe, we recommend serving food on separate dishes. The plates would be perfect party favors for your muses.

When stamping on a curved surface, you may need to rock the stamp back and forth to transfer the image successfully.

fig. a

What's All the Buzz?

THIS IS ONE PROJECT YOU CAN DO ON THE FLY.

You'll BEE so happy that this quick and easy project takes just minutes—really!

Pour a very small amount of crafts glass paint on a paper plate and use a paintbrush to spread it into a thin layer. Press the stamp into the paint and test on the plate. Once you are satisfied, press the stamp into the paint again and then carefully onto the vase. Remove and let dry.

YOU'LL NEED:

_Crafts glass paint

_Paper plate

_Paintbrush

_Rubber stamp

_Vase

Dishing It
LET A LITTLE BIRDIE JOIN YOU FOR DINNER.

Dress up plain dishware for a truly original tablescape. Use the same motif at each setting or vary them to really make things interesting.

Use the pattern on page 204 to create a stencil. Use stencil adhesive to secure the stencil to the plate. Use a stencil brush and glass paint to stencil the bird to the plate. Remove the stencil, then dab blue and green dots around the bird using a paintbrush. Let dry, then bake according to the paint manufacturer's instructions to set the paint.

YOU'LL NEED:

_Bird pattern

_Stencil adhesive

_Stencil plastic

_Crafts knife

_Stencil brush

_Crafts glass paint

_Paintbrush

_Ceramic dishware

_Oven

For a matching napkin, shrink and reverse the stencil and use fabric paints to stencil the image.

be merry.

drink

YOU'LL NEED:

_Stencil adhesive

_Letter stencils

_Ceramic dishware

_Stencil brush

_Crafts glass paint

_Oven

Conversation Pieces

LET CHEERY DISHES SAY WHAT'S ON YOUR MIND.

Dressing up plain dishware with simple words or phrases makes your table settings something worth talking about.

Use stencil adhesive to secure stencils to the plate. Use a stencil brush and glass paint to stencil letters on the plate. Remove the stencils. Let dry, then bake according to the paint manufacturer's instructions to set the paint.

glass

Pretty Little Things

GIVE GLASS BOTTLES A BOOST OF COLOR.

Sometimes the littlest things bring a big smile. These happy additions are an instant perk-up to any countertop or windowsill.

YOU'LL NEED:

_Glass bottles

_Rubbing alcohol

_Enamel glass paint

_Paper towels

1. Clean bottles inside and out and let dry. To prime, pour rubbing alcohol into each bottle (**fig. a**) and rotate to coat the inside surface. Pour out excess and let dry.

2. Pour enamel paint into each bottle, tapping and rotating to coat entire surface (**fig. b**).

3. Place the bottles upside down on paper towels and let dry overnight (**fig. c**).

diy tip

If your enamel paint is too thick to swirl around and coat the inside of the bottle, follow the manufacturer's directions for thinning it.

fig. a

fig. b

fig. c

THE PALETTE:
the bright side

This eye-popping palette calls for lively shades of green and blue. The sassy hues play well together, especially when grounded by crisp white.

Front and center, clear aqua blue flaunts a confident attitude.

This sour apple green shade almost makes you pucker.

A brilliant cobalt hue adds depth to the lighter tones.

A whiter than white canvas enhances the vivid hues.

Dotted Drinkware

FRESHEN THINGS UP WITH A FAUX FROSTED LOOK.

Tired of plain glassware? Serve up a refreshing redo with stickers and glass paint.

YOU'LL NEED:

_Glassware

_Sticker labels

_Foam spouncer

_White glass paint

Clean the glass and let dry. Apply circle label stickers as desired. Use a foam spouncer to apply white glass paint over the labels and up the sides of the glass (**fig. a**). Peel the stickers off while the paint is still wet (**fig. b**) and scratch off any paint that seeped underneath. Let dry.

fig. a

fig. b

Avoid getting paint on the rim of the pitcher or glass where it might be ingested when used.

Frost Fancy

TRY THIS EASY METHOD FOR ENHANCING GLASS.

Forget about messy etching creams. Now you can get the same look by using a special glass paint in a spray can.

Use painter's tape in various widths to mask a combination of stripes and rectangles on glass vases. Coat the glass with frosted-glass spray paint, following the manufacturer's directions. When dry, remove the tape to reveal your patterns.

YOU'LL NEED:

_Glass vases

_Painter's tape

_Frosted-glass spray
  paint

Mirror Image

GLAM THINGS UP WITH SILVERED GLASS.

When sprayed on the reverse side of clear glass, Looking Glass paint gives the appearance of mercury glass.

YOU'LL NEED:

_Glass lamp base

_Looking Glass
 spray paint

Following the paint manufacturer's directions, spray several light coats of Looking Glass paint on the inside of a glass lamp base. The wider the opening of the glass base, the easier it is to coat the inside surface. If you prefer the look of vintage mercury glass, you can achieve a more mottled reflection by first applying water to the surface, then painting over it while still wet.

Shimmer and Shine

ADD A LITTLE SPARKLE TO BASIC VOTIVES.

A metallic touch offers a festive glint at the holidays or any time of year, especially when near flickering candlelight.

Use scrapbooking stickers to create designs on plain glass votives and hurricanes. In a well-ventilated area, spray the glass with silver metallic paint. When dry, peel off the stickers. Pair with other sparkly accessories such as rhinestones or glass stones.

YOU'LL NEED:

_Glass votives and
  hurricanes
_Stickers
_Silver metallic
  spray paint

Mirror, Mirror on the Wall

THIS EASY TREATMENT JUST MIGHT BE THE FAIREST OF THEM ALL.

Get the charming look of vintage etched mirrors **(fig. a)** using inexpensive frosted-glass spray.

YOU'LL NEED:

_Stencil

_Stencil adhesive

_Mirror

_Painter's tape

_Kraft paper

_Frosted-glass
  spray paint

1. Spray stencil back with stencil adhesive and adhere to mirror in the desired location. Use painter's tape and kraft paper to mask off all other areas to protect from overspray.

2. Spray the stencil opening with a light mist of frosted-glass spray paint. When partially dry, remove the stencil and masking. Let dry completely.

fig. a

152

fig. a

fig. b

diytip To get a smoother flow of paint for small, detailed lettering, slightly water down the paint and use a lettering brush to apply.

Label Lovers

THESE CAN-DO CANISTERS PRETTY UP A COUNTERTOP.

Not only are labels an easy way to embellish plain-Jane canisters, but they assure no one will accidentally pour sugar into the salt!

1. Using a computer and printer, print words to fit the canister width. Cut the paper with words into strips that fit inside the canisters and tape into place (**fig. a**).

2. Using a small paintbrush and glass paint, carefully trace the printed words (**fig. b**). Let dry.

YOU'LL NEED:

_Computer, printer, paper

_Scissors

_Glass canisters

_Tape

_Paintbrush

_Glass paint

This desk is supported by a pair of metal sawhorses. Their original bright orange hue was painted over with electric blue.

Precious Metals

ORGANIZE IN STYLE WITH A PAINTED METAL CADDY.

A hardworking tool tote moves off the garage floor and into the home office as a prettied-up storage-savvy desk caddy.

YOU'LL NEED:

_Metal tool tote

_Wire brush

_Rubber gloves

_Towel

_Bleach water

_Rust-inhibiting primer

_Spray paint

_Pattern

_Stencil plastic

_Crafts knife

_Stencil adhesive

_Foam spouncer

_Crafts paints

_Artist's brush

_Polyurethane

diy tip If you don't have a steady hand, clean the stencil well and use it and a foam spouncer to apply the contrasting spot color.

1. Remove any loose paint or rust with a wire brush. Wearing rubber gloves, clean the metal thoroughly using a towel and a combination of 3 parts bleach to 1 part water. Let dry.

2. Apply two coats of rust-inhibiting primer, letting dry between coats. When dry, spray paint yellow. Let dry.

3. Using the pattern on page 204, cut a stencil from stencil plastic. Spray the back of the stencil with stencil adhesive and adhere to the caddy. Use a foam spouncer to apply the stencil to the caddy using orange-yellow crafts paint (**fig. a**). Carefully reposition the stencil as needed. Remove the stencil and let dry.

4. Using an artist's brush and a contrasting color of crafts paint, handpaint two or three sections of the stencil (**fig. b**). Let dry. Top with polyurethane if desired.

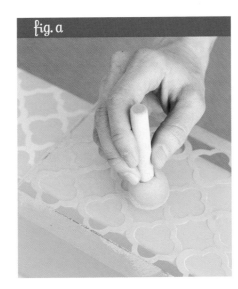
fig. a

fig. b

THE PALETTE:
shock therapy

Electric hues are just the thing to keep you wide awake at work and play. With an energized scheme like this, there's no chance of boredom setting in.

Feeling blue? Give your room a jolt with this vibrant hue.

Lots of eye-popping yellow is sure to recharge your space.

Orange-yellow hues play second fiddle as an accent here.

Keep enough white in sight to settle this powerful palette down.

Crystal Cheer

PRETTY PAINTS PERK UP AN OLD CHANDELIER.

Ho-hum chandeliers are easy to find at flea markets and thrift shops. A tarnished brass fixture was anything but beautiful, but with most of the crystals intact, it was a perfect candidate for a remake.

YOU'LL NEED:

_Chandelier

_Wire brush

_Rubber gloves

_Towel

_Bleach water

_Rust-inhibiting primer spray

_Latex or oil base paint

_Paintbrush

_Glass paint

1. Remove all crystals, bulbs, and candle sleeves. Remove any loose paint or rust with a wire brush. Wearing rubber gloves, clean old metal pieces thoroughly using a towel and a combination of 3 parts bleach to 1 part water. Let dry.

2. Spray with a rust-inhibiting primer, then paint with the desired color. Let dry.

3. Clean the glass crystals, then use a paintbrush and glass paint to paint one side of each crystal. Let dry, then fasten to the chandelier. Replace the candle sleeves and bulbs.

For additional color or pattern, use pretty paper to cover the candle sleeves. This works best on smooth sleeves without decorative wax drips.

YOU'LL NEED:

_Metal chairs

_Wire brush

_Rubber gloves

_Towel

_Bleach water

_Rust-inhibiting primer

_Spray paint in yellow
and cream

_Painter's tape

Sunny Seats
STRIPES STAND THE TEST OF TIME.

Yellowware color and stripes—a country style favorite—are translated onto a vintage metal porch chair using paint and DIY pride.

1. Remove any loose paint or rust with a wire brush. Wearing rubber gloves, clean old metal pieces thoroughly using a towel and a combination of 3 parts bleach to 1 part water. Let dry.

2. Apply two coats of rust-inhibiting primer, letting dry between coats. When dry, paint with yellow paint. Let dry. Use painter's tape to mask the stripes, then fill in with cream paint. Let dry.

Making Waves

IT'S SUNNY SIDE UP FOR THIS CHARMING CART.

Metal rolling carts like these are a dime a dozen at any flea market. See beyond the weathered surface and know that a quick paint makeover will give it a bright new face.

YOU'LL NEED:

_Metal cart

_Wire brush

_Rubber gloves

_Towel

_Bleach water

_Rust-inhibiting
  primer

_Semigloss latex
  paint in light and
  dark yellow

_Paintbrush

_Plastic container

_Glaze medium

_Combing tool

1. Remove any loose paint or rust with a wire brush. Wearing rubber gloves, clean the metal thoroughly using a towel and a combination of 3 parts bleach to 1 part water. Let dry.

2. Apply two coats of rust-inhibiting primer, letting dry between coats. When dry, paint light yellow. Let dry.

3. In a plastic container, mix 1 part dark yellow paint with 4 parts glaze medium. Brush the mixture on the cart's two shelves and, while wet, drag the combing tool through it using a waving motion to create the playful design. Let dry.

Served Up in Style

THIS STYLISH TRAY IS ANYTHING BUT THE BLUES.

While old metal relics are fun to freshen up, don't overlook new items such as recent-issue trays printed with promotional logos.

1. Apply two coats of rust-inhibiting primer, letting dry between coats. When dry, spray the tray a relaxing gray-blue hue. Let dry.

2. Pour a small amount of white crafts paint on a paper plate. Dip a foam crafts stamp into the paint and press lightly to a paper towel to dab off excess paint before pressing to the tray. Repeat until satisfied with the stamped pattern. For a partial stamp design at the corners, cut a second stamp in half on the diagonal and repeat the stamping process. Add dot details using a paintbrush.

YOU'LL NEED:

_Metal tray

_Rust-inhibiting primer

_Blue spray paint

_White crafts paint

_Paper plate

_2 identical foam stamps

_Paper towel

_Paintbrush

Light the Way

BRIGHT WHITE IS A SUREFIRE RESCUE FOR TARNISHED TREASURES.

Buried under a heap of castoffs in an old shed, this lamp might never again have seen the light of day. But with paint to the rescue, it once again shines bright.

YOU'LL NEED:

_Metal lamp

_Wire brush

_Rubber gloves

_Towel

_Bleach water

_Rust-inhibiting
  primer

_White spray paint

_Oil paint marker

1. Remove any loose paint or rust with a wire brush. Wearing rubber gloves, clean the metal thoroughly using a towel and a combination of 3 parts bleach to 1 part water. Let dry.

2. Apply two coats of rust-inhibiting primer, letting dry between coats. When dry, paint white. Let dry.

3. Using an oil paint marker, fill in the depressions in the lamp's metal base **(fig. a)**. Let dry.

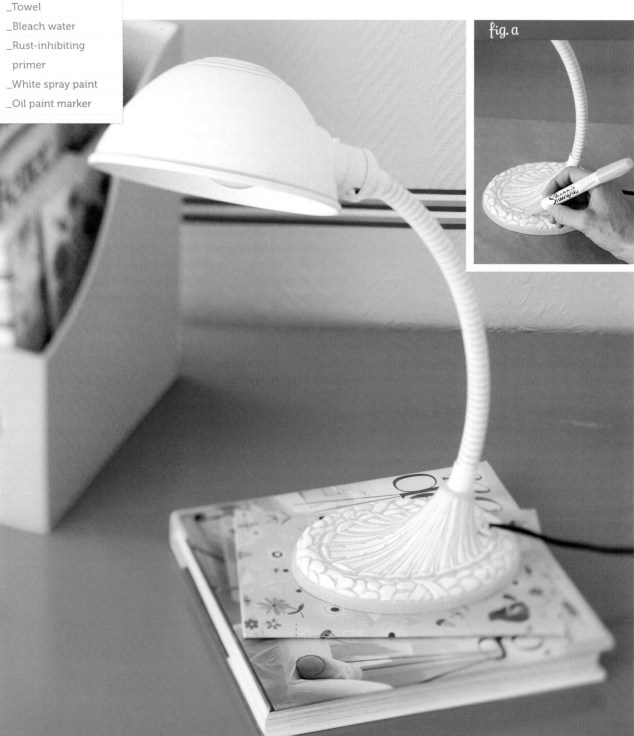

fig. a

If you can't find a notched squeegee, purchase a regular one and use a utility knife to cut notches in it.

fig. a

YOU'LL NEED:

_Metal lockers

_Wire brush

_Rubber gloves

_Towel

_Bleach water

_Rust-inhibiting
 oil-base primer

_Blue oil-base paint

_Painter's tape

_Cream latex paint

_Notched squeegee

Back to School
THIS LOCKER REDO IS WELCOME HOMEWORK.

A school remodel meant a slew of old metal lockers were on the auction block. This set gets an easy update to make it porch-worthy.

1. Remove any loose paint or rust with a wire brush. Wearing rubber gloves, clean the metal thoroughly using a towel and a combination of 3 parts bleach to 1 part water. Let dry.

2. Apply two coats of rust-inhibiting oil-base primer, letting dry between coats. When dry, paint with blue oil-base paint. Let dry for 48 hours.

3. Use painter's tape to mask off the door front. Apply a coat of cream paint and, while wet, use a notched squeegee, running the tool first horizontally then vertically for a woven look (**fig. a**).

Chapter 6

PAINT PROJECTS FOR

cabinetry & tile

cabinetry

tile

PAGES 164–171   PAGES 172–177

cabinetry

A bold hue with an aged finish gives this kitchen a comfortable, country look. A simple stencil lends cabinet doors personality.

Aged to Perf[...]

GIVE BORING CABINETS THE BRUSH-[...]

A few easy steps give dark and dated kitchen c[...]
and wooden furniture feet and you've got a ne[...]

YOU'LL NEED:

_Cotton rags
_Mild detergent
_180-grit sandpaper
_Tack cloth
_Paintbrush
_Primer
_Semigloss latex
 paints
_Plastic container
_Glaze medium
_Flower pattern
_Stencil plastic
_Crafts knife
_Stencil adhesive
_Crafts paint
_Stencil brush

1. Remove c[...]
   with wate[...]
   fine sandp[...]

2. Sand again[...]

3. Paint using[...]

4. In a plastic c[...]
   hue. Brush th[...]
   if off, leaving[...]

5. Use the patter[...]
   stencil adhesiv[...]
   stencil. Let dry[...]

Amazing Glaze

FOR THIS LOOK, ADD WOOD APPLIQUÉS AN[...]

Inspired by traditional Wedgwood pottery, these
perfectly classic cornflower blue.

YOU'LL NEED:

_Cotton rags
_Mild detergent
_180-grit sa[...]
_Tack cl[...]
_Se[...]

div tip For a smoother finish, apply primer and top coat using a paint sprayer rather than a brush or roller.

fig. a

fig. b

fig. c

fig. d

...D A WORN FINISH.

...cabinets go from a cabbage green hue to

1. Remove cabinet doors, hinges, knobs, and pulls. Clean, sand, and prime the cabinets according to the instructions on page 165.

2. Sand again and wipe with a tack cloth.

3. Paint using two coats of the desired color of latex paint in a semigloss finish, letting dry between coats.

4. Using wood glue, adhere cream-painted wood appliqués to the corners and center of the cabinet door. Brush burnt umber glaze over the cabinet surface (**fig. a**), then rub the surface with a rag (**fig. b**), working it in to create the desired worn look. Let dry for several days before reinstalling the doors on the cabinets.

...dpaper

...oth

...migloss latex paint

_Paintbrushes

_Wood appliqués

_Wood glue

_Burnt umber glaze

diy tip For less emphasis on the wood appliqués, try painting them a slightly darker or lighter tone of the cabinet color so they have less contrast.

fig. a

fig. b

A Lift for Laminate

YES, LAMINATE CAN BE PAINTED!

If you're stuck with dated laminate cabinets, never fear. The right paint product and new hardware treat them to a whole new look.

1. Remove cabinet doors, hinges, knobs, and pulls. Clean and sand the cabinets according to the instructions on page 165.

2. Apply a primer formulated specifically for laminate or slick surfaces. A shellac-base primer smells for about an hour and requires ammonia for cleaning tools, but it cures quickly, speeding up your project. Let dry according to the manufacturer's directions.

3. Use a paint roller or sprayer to apply the desired top coat and let dry. The top coat you select will depend on whether you used an oil- or latex-base primer. The cure time before reinstalling the doors will depend on the primer and top coat products used. Be sure to follow the manufacturer's directions.

You can paint laminate countertops as well. Just be sure to use a water-base, two-part epoxy paint made for the job.

Shopping
- milk
- apples
- bread
- berries
- eggs
- sugar

diy tip If a black hue is too daring for you, look for chalkboard paints in other colors or make your own using 6 parts acrylic paint, 3 parts water-base glazing medium, and 1 part unsanded powder tile grout.

fig. a

Chalk About It

CHALKBOARD PAINT GRADUATES FROM CLASSROOM TO KITCHEN.

Turn one or more cabinet fronts into a memo board to record shopping lists, doodles, or don't-forgets. You can even install a door pull upside down to hold chalk.

1. Remove cabinet doors, hinges, knobs, and pulls. Clean, sand, and prime the cabinets according to the instructions on page 165. Base-coat the cabinet doors with green paint and let dry.

2. Tape off the door panel with painter's tape. Spray the panel with chalkboard paint **(fig. a)**, following the manufacturer's directions. Remove the painter's tape and let dry for several days before reinstalling the doors on the cabinets.

YOU'LL NEED:

_Cotton rags

_Mild detergent

_180-grit sandpaper

_Tack cloth

_Green spray paint

_Painter's tape

_Black chalkboard paint

Lovely Lattice

BE INSPIRED BY GEOMETRIC PATTERNS.

Masking intersecting lines makes for a bold yet easy-to-do cabinet remake.

YOU'LL NEED:

_Cotton rags

_Mild detergent

_180-grit sandpaper

_Tack cloth

_Paintbrush

_Primer

_White semigloss
  latex paint

_¾-inch-wide
  electrical tape

_Ruler

_Aqua semigloss
  latex paint

1. Remove cabinet doors, hinges, knobs, and pulls. Clean, sand, and prime cabinets according to the instructions on page 165. Base-coat the cabinet doors with white paint and let dry.

2. Using electrical tape and a ruler, create a lattice design, starting with the vertical and horizontal lines, then intersecting with diagonals as shown *below*. Paint the cabinet doors aqua blue.

3. Peel off the electrical tape before completely dry **(fig. a)**. Let dry for several days before reinstalling the doors on the cabinets.

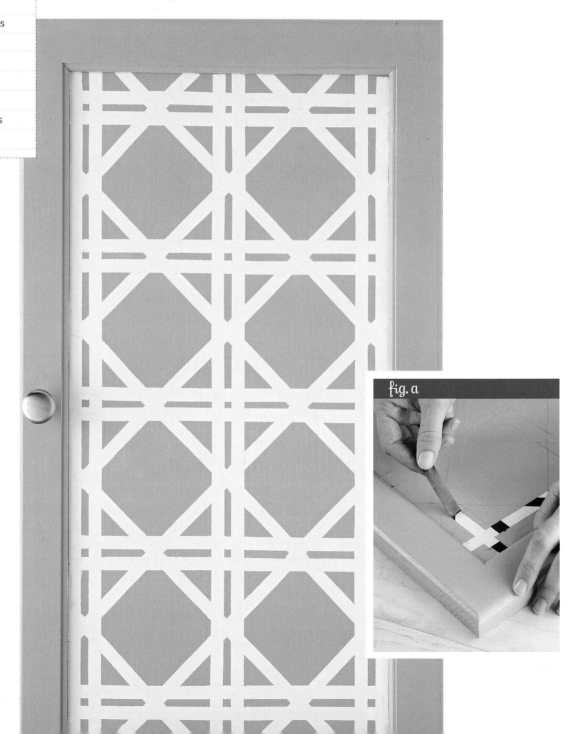

fig. a

170

fig. a

Artistic Endeavor

LET CABINET DOORS BE A CANVAS FOR ARTLIKE ACCENTS.

Add this easy embellishment to the front of every cabinet door or to just a few focal-point ones. The border adds a frame element to the creative masterpiece.

1. Remove cabinet doors, hinges, knobs, and pulls. Clean, sand, and prime the cabinets according to the instructions on page 165. Base-coat the cabinet doors with white paint and let dry.

2. Spray stencil adhesive on the stencil, then center it on the cabinet door, pressing firmly. Use a stencil brush and crafts paint to pounce paint over the design (**fig. a**), removing the stencil when covered.

3. Tape off the border using painter's tape and use an artist's brush to paint a coordinating border. Remove the tape and let dry for several days before reinstalling the doors on the cabinets.

After peeling off petal stickers, you may need to scrape paint that has seeped underneath or add paint where it pulled off with the sticker.

Tile Transformer

A MODERN MOTIF GIVES PLAIN TILE ROOM TO BLOOM.

Underutilized and begging for attention, the side of this kitchen cabinet was a perfect canvas for an unusual art endeavor. Rather than paint right on the cabinet surface, we tiled it first so the art would have a gridded look.

YOU'LL NEED:

_Nonsoapy
  detergent

_Denatured alcohol

_Patterns

_Stencil plastic

_Crafts knife

_Sticker paper

_Painter's tape

_3-piece foam
  spouncer set

_Enamel crafts
  paints

_Artist's brush

1. Clean tile with a nonsoapy detergent; let dry. Remove any remaining surface residue with denatured alcohol. Using the patterns on page 205, cut four stencils from stencil plastic (large leaf, small leaf, green ring section, and pink/brown ring section) and cut eight petal shapes from sticker paper.

2. Use painter's tape to secure the first stencil in place. Using a large foam spouncer, stencil the dark and light green sections with enamel crafts paints. Remove the stencil and let dry. Use the artist's brush to fill in the grout lines with paint. Let dry.

3. Place the flower center petal stickers in the center of the flower. Tape the second stencil in place. Use the large spouncer to stencil the pink flower section (**fig. a**), then the brown section. Remove the stencil and let dry. Fill in the grout lines with paint (**fig. b**). Let dry. Peel off the petal stickers (**fig. c**).

4. Tape off the flower stem with painter's tape and use the spouncer to stencil with green paint. Remove the tape and let dry. Stencil the large and small leaf shapes using dark green paint, fill in the grout lines, and let dry. Hand-paint the center of each leaf with light green paint. Use three sizes of foam spouncers and brown paint to make scattered dots (**fig. d**). Let dry.

fig. a

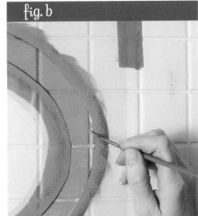

fig. b

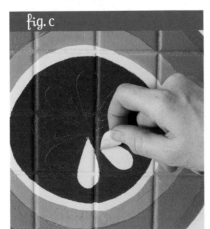

fig. c

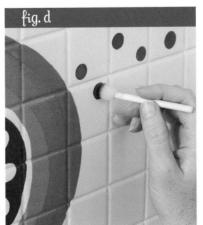

fig. d

Music to Your Ears
CREATE A QUARTET OF COASTERS.

This easy-to-paint ceramic tile set is sure to hit the right note with guests. Choose musical motifs or another theme to suit your fancy.

YOU'LL NEED:

_Desired clip art

_Pencil

_White ceramic tiles

_Carbon paper
  (optional)

_Paintbrush

_Porcelain paint

_Rubber cabinet
  bumpers

1. Download and resize free clip art of instruments or desired motif.

2. Print out, then shade the shapes with a pencil (**fig. a**). Flip the patterns over and use a pencil to trace around them, transfering the outline of the image to simple white tiles (or use carbon paper to transfer the images).

3. Using a thin paintbrush and porcelain paint, fill in or paint around each silhouette (**fig. b**). Let dry.

4. Attach rubber cabinet bumpers to the backs of the tiles to protect surfaces and keep the coasters from shifting.

fig. a

fig. b

THE PALETTE:
modern day

Aqua and orange hues lend midcentury modern appeal to a variety of spaces, especially when paired with modern accents like these silhouettes.

Forward-looking and fresh, let aqua dominate modern spaces.

A little orange goes a long way, so limit the hue to accents.

Though not shown, try adding chocolate brown to this scheme.

White helps contrasting silhouettes look crisp and neat.

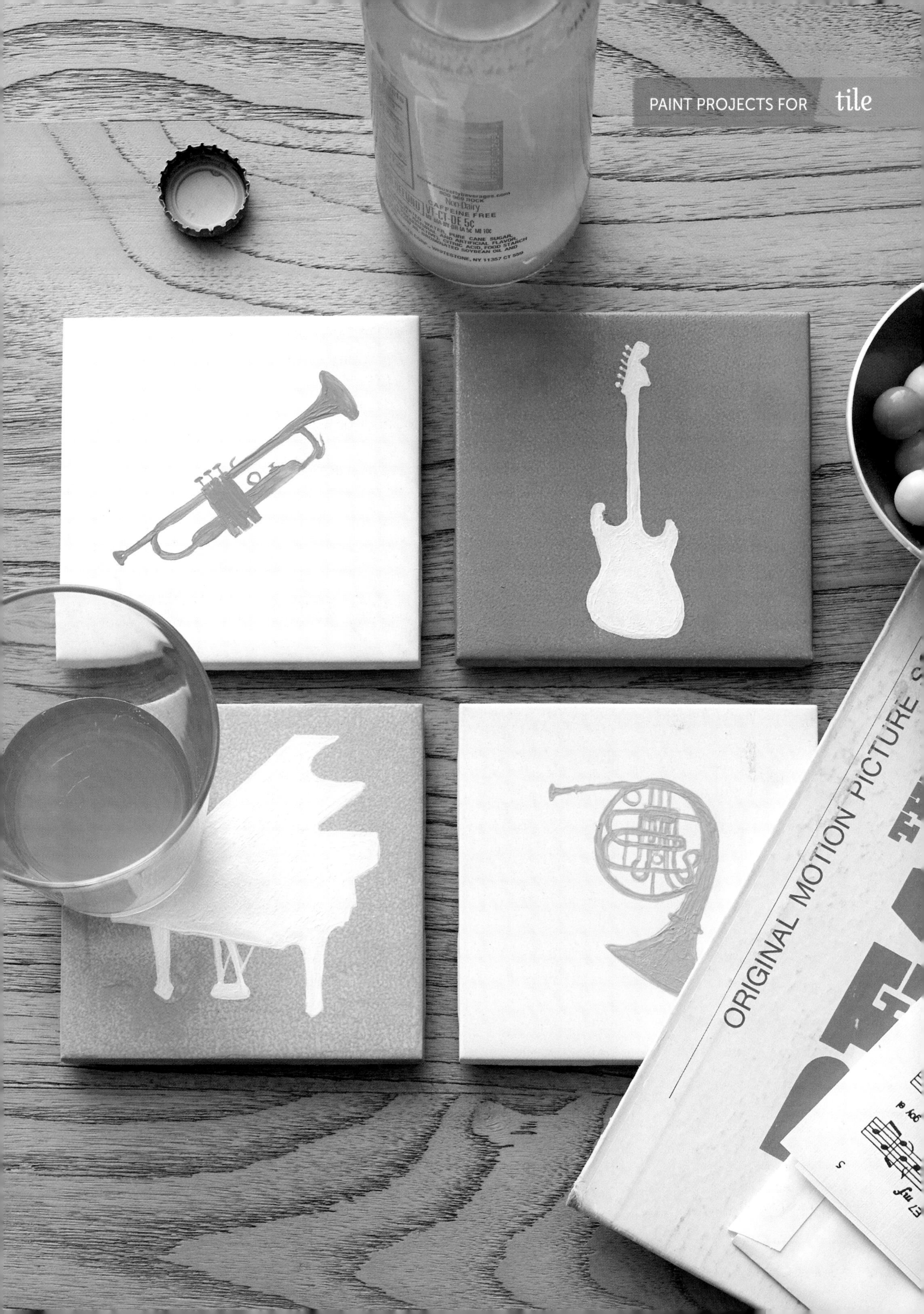
Non-Dairy
CAFFEINE FREE
ORIGINAL MOTION PICTURE

Cheery Checker

A LITTLE PAINT ADDS CLASSIC COUNTRY CHARM.

Though it'll take a little patience to tape off this checkerboard pattern, the transformation from plain-Jane to perfectly delightful is well worth the effort!

YOU'LL NEED:

_Nonsoapy
  detergent

_Denatured alcohol

_Painter's tape

_Enamel crafts paints

_Foam brush

_Artist's brush

1. Clean tiles according to the instructions on page 173. Use painter's tape to tape off a 4-inch square in the upper right corner of each 8-inch-square tile. Paint red using enamel crafts paint and a foam brush. Let dry, then remove the tape. Repeat the taping and painting process on the lower left corners of tiles.

2. Use an artist's brush to handpaint flowers and dotted diamonds as shown in **(fig. a)**.

fig. a

For whole apples, use painter's tape to mask off the core before stenciling.

fig. a

YOU'LL NEED:

_Nonsoapy detergent
_Denatured alcohol
_Apple pattern
_Stencil plastic
_Crafts knife
_Stencil adhesive
_Glass paint
_Foam spouncer
_Artist's brush
_Painter's tape

An Apple a Day
GIVE A BACKSPLASH A SUBTLE SPLASH OF PAINT.

Randomly placed apple motifs offer interest to solid green glass tiles.

1. Clean tiles according to the instructions on page 173. Use the pattern on page 205 to cut a stencil from stencil plastic.

2. Spray the stencil back with stencil adhesive and adhere to tile. Use glass paint and a foam spouncer to stencil the design. Remove the stencil and let dry.

3. Use an artist's brush to apply the stem and seed details **(fig. a)**. Let dry.

tips, tools & techniques

Top 15 Tips

Using today's paints and paint tools, you can add delightful and durable color all around the house. Tried and true, these insightful tips will ensure you do the job right—and just might save you a few do-overs in the process.

1 Test your color before committing to gallons of a particular shade. Most companies sell small quantities for testing. Paint a piece of white poster board and tape the board to the wall in the room you are planning to paint. Observe the color throughout the day as the light changes. Live with the color for a few days, moving the board to other walls in the room. If you still love the color, you're ready to move ahead with confidence.

2. Quality brushes apply paint in a thick, smooth film. Examine a brush for a good taper, with bristles in the center slightly longer than those at the edge. The bristles should be at least half as long as they are wide and should be bound with a rust-resistant metal ferrule that is nailed on, not just crimped to the handle. Look for a well-shaped bare wood handle large enough to grip comfortably.

3. There's a difference between dry time, when a paint is dry to the touch, and cure time, when it's truly durable. It can take several days to weeks for paint to fully cure. Humididty can keep paint from drying and curing as quickly as the paint label says.

4 To determine whether a painted surface was painted with an oil- or water-base paint, soak a cotton ball in ammonia and stick it to the surface using painter's tape. Remove after an hour; if the painted surface has wrinkles, it's water-base paint. If it doesn't, it's oil-base.

5. Choose the right roller cover for the job: For a smooth surface, choose a short nap or pile. Rougher surfaces require a longer nap. And the higher the gloss level of the paint, the shorter the nap of the roller cover should be.

6 When using more than 1 gallon of paint, mix all gallons together in a 5-gallon bucket. Called boxing, this procedure will ensure that the color is uniform throughout the application. Boxing is particularly worthwhile if you're using a custom-mixed color.

7. Apply no more than 8–10 inches of painter's tape at a time to be certain of a straight edge. Smooth the edges with a putty knife. Wait until the paint is dry to the touch and remove the tape slowly at a 45-degree angle. If the tape begins to tear, run a crafts knife along the seam to loosen it from the dried paint.

12 Many paint manufacturers offer Earth-friendly options with fewer harmful chemicals and more natural ingredients.

8 When you take a break from your paint job, wrap your brushes and rollers in plastic bags, squeezing the air out, and seal with twist-ties or rubber bands. To leave them overnight, place the sealed tools in the refrigerator.

9. Painted surfaces can stick together if they come into contact before the paint dries completely. Dark colors stick more than light ones, and glossy paints stick more than flat ones. If windows, doors, or other surfaces stick after the paint dries, rub them with talcum powder to minimize the problem.

10 When sealing a painted surface, use an oil-base sealer over oil-base paint. Both oil- and latex-base sealers can be used over latex paint.

11. If painting a ceiling, paint it before painting the walls. Use a roller with a telescoping handle and paint the first coat in the same direction as the major light source (such as a window) and a second coat perpendicular to the light. When repainting a white ceiling white, it can be difficult to see what you've painted. Look for ceiling paint that goes on light pink or blue and then dries to a white finish.

13. Paint your room from the top to the bottom. Start with the ceiling, then the walls, then windows, doors, and other woodwork, finishing with the baseboards. Cut in with a 2-inch strip around the edges of the ceiling, start painting in a corner, and then paint according to tip #11. Before painting your walls, cut in along all the edges, around door and window frames, and along the baseboards. Apply the paint to the walls with a roller.

14. Avoid painting over wallpaper, but if you absolutely can't remove it first, here are some steps to follow: First, wash the wall with a wet sponge; let dry. Use wallpaper paste to secure any loose edges or seams. Using a roller cover with a 3/16- or 1/4-inch nap, roll on tinted shellac-base stain-blocking primer; let dry 24 hours. To finish, apply two coats of paint.

15. Store paint successfully by keeping air out of the paint container. To accomplish this, add a gasket between the cover and the can using a circle cut from a heavy-duty trash bag. Spray vegetable oil on one side of the bag and set it on the can with the lid on top of the plastic. Tap the lid to seat it in the well. Store the can upside down in a room free from temperature extremes.

The Right Stuff

If you're going to put in the effort to paint something, you want good results. And the best way to ensure that is to have the right tools on hand. They will save you time and effort and reduce frustration. Select the best quality you can afford; the right tools will see you through years of successful painting projects.

CANVAS DROP CLOTHS
Canvas drop cloths absorb liquid and are heavy enough to stay put when used on the floor or over furnishings. A tight weave offers the best protection.

PLASTIC DROP CLOTHS
Plastic drop cloths are inexpensive and protect surfaces. However, they don't absorb paint, can be slippery, and may shift easily.

LINT-FREE CLOTHS
Use lint-free cloths to remove dirt and dust, clean up spills, wipe away mistakes, or manipulate glaze techniques.

STIR STICKS
Grab free sticks when you buy paint. Stir paint thoroughly and frequently to keep the color evenly mixed.

3-INCH BRUSH
Good for outlining walls and ceilings and for painting large areas, this brush is a workhorse. Look for a bare wood handle to get the best grip. Hold it between your thumb and fingers in a relaxed grip.

ANGLED BRUSH
This is the best tool for painting door and window frames, moldings, and other areas where you need more control. Hold this brush like a pencil.

HOUSEHOLD BRUSH
This brush is ideal for painting small areas, furnishings, or accent pieces.

FOAM BRUSH
Disposable foam brushes come in several sizes for smaller paint and crafts projects.

ARTIST'S BRUSHES
These are perfect for detail work and freehand designs on small furnishings and accent pieces.

STENCIL BRUSHES
Stencil brushes are available in a variety of sizes. Use large ones for overall coverage and small ones to fill in details.

WEAVER BRUSH
A weaver brush is used to create the look of linen or denim.

Specialty painter's tape is used to mask off areas before painting. Medium-adhesion tape is often used on woodwork that has a nonporous finish, such as gloss or semigloss paint. It adheres and seals well and will stay put for the duration of the project. If left on too long, however, it may pull off the finish when removed. Low-tack painter's tape for delicate surfaces is used to temporarily mask off stripes, borders, and wall panels. It is often removed immediately after painting. Its mild adhesive will not pull off paint when removed. Both types of tape are available in a variety of widths.

roller cover roundup

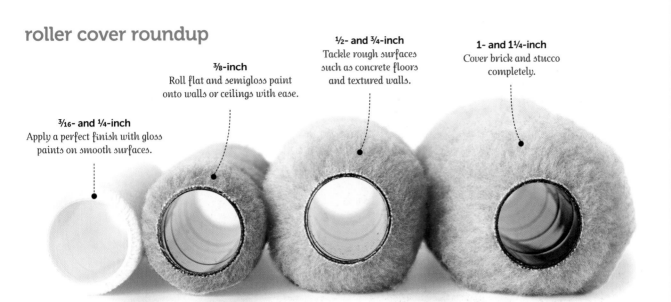

³/₁₆- and ¼-inch
Apply a perfect finish with gloss paints on smooth surfaces.

³/₈-inch
Roll flat and semigloss paint onto walls or ceilings with ease.

½- and ¾-inch
Tackle rough surfaces such as concrete floors and textured walls.

1- and 1¼-inch
Cover brick and stucco completely.

EXTENSION HANDLE
Extend the reach of your paint roller to make painting easier on high walls and ceilings.

ROLLER COVERS
Use a polyester cover to apply latex paints and lamb's wool for oil-base paints. Covers come in various naps as shown above.

MINI ROLLER
Mini rollers make it easy to paint small areas and are ideal for getting into tight corners.

ROLLER
Rollers will spread about three times as much paint as a brush in the same amount of time.

ROLLER TRAY AND LINER
A metal roller tray holds paint that will be applied with a roller. Look for sturdy construction with a deep well. Also pick up disposable liners to make cleanup and color changes easier. When you've finished painting, let the leftover paint dry in the liner before throwing it away.

PAINT PAD
Made of foam or nylon, pads are ideal for a clean line, particularly in hard-to-reach spaces and corners where rollers won't fit.

TRIM GUIDE
Try this tool when painting trim edges against walls. It also protects flooring when painting baseboards.

CHECK ROLLER
After a weaver brush establishes the basic warp and weft pattern, a check roller is rolled vertically and horizontally through the glaze to create the look of faded threads on a denim fabric.

TRIANGLE COMB
Combing tools create fine pinstripes when run through a top coat of glaze. Smaller combs may be purchased and large ones may be homemade from a squeegee.

WOOD-GRAINING TOOL
A wood-graining tool, pulled through wet glaze using a drag-and-rock motion, creates the look of knotty wood planks.

LONG LEVEL
A long carpenter's level helps accurately mark long lines. Look for a level with printed measurements to measure and mark at the same time.

SANDING BLOCK, SANDPAPER
Available in medium, fine, and very fine grits, they smooth repaired walls and increase tooth for the application of new paint.

PAINT CAN OPENER
A metal paint can opener is an essential—and usually free—tool to open paint cans easily without ruining the lid.

SCRAPER
Use this rigid blade to apply and smooth wall compound on a large area or to retape wallboard joints. It also can be used to remove old paint and wallpaper.

PUTTY KNIFE
A flexible-blade putty knife is useful for filling nail holes or open joints in molding and frames with wood putty or spackling compound.

5-IN-1 TOOL
A multipurpose tool like this helps open paint cans, scrape narrow areas, apply compound, and remove excess paint when cleaning rollers.

working with paint chips

Paint chips are much more than little cards of color. They organize paint collections from a single manufacturer, provide a look at tints and shades of the same color, and help you find coordinating hues. Learn how to talk about color using these common terms. Then put it all together as you study paint cards.

VALUE
Value is the lightness or darkness of a color. Sky blue is a light value; cobalt is a dark value. Paint chip cards typically have light and dark variations of one color. Use light yellow in one room, for example, and a deeper hue from the same paint-chip card in an adjoining room. For delineation, pick colors separated by at least one chip on a card.

TINT
Closest to white in value, tints are also called pastels. You'll find them on the top of a paint card or in a separate collection of whites and off-whites. Tints can appear almost white or stronger in hue.

INTENSITY
This term refers to color saturation and specifies clearness or brightness. Adding white, black, or a complementary color to a pure color diminishes its intensity. To ensure the same intensity for contrasting colors, select hues from the same position on paint chip cards, using the same paint brand.

SHADE
Darkening or dulling colors with black or gray creates shades of that color. Shades can be near the top of the paint card or at the very bottom.

POUR SPOUTS FOR GALLON CANS

Plastic pour spouts clip onto standard gallon cans of paint and enable easy pouring.

PRIMER

Primers penetrate unpainted surfaces, create a uniform skin for your paint, and can also inhibit stains. Tint your primer if you are painting a dark color over light or light over dark.

TRIM PAINT

The hard and durable enamel finish stands up to constant contact and frequent cleaning.

INTERIOR PAINT

Latex paints are the best all-around paints for interiors. Low-odor, fast-drying latex has a water base and is easy to clean up.

GLASS/TILE PAINT

Formulated for use on hard, slick surfaces, this paint offers one-coat coverage and is top-rack dishwasher safe.

FABRICS PAINT

Imbued with a textile medium, these paints will withstand laundering. Test the paint on a fabric scrap before painting.

SPRAY PAINT

Available for many applications, spray paints come in a variety of colors and finishes.

DECORATIVE GLAZE

Decorative glazes mix with paints to help achieve a variety of decorative finishes. Some of the more common glazes are pearlescent, opalescent, metallic, and antique.

STENCIL ACETATE

Stencil acetate or plastic is used to create custom stencils. Just draw your design and cut it out using a crafts knife or scissors.

SPRAY ADHESIVE

Adhere stencils to a wall or other surface using repositionable adhesive spray, reapplying as needed.

POLYURETHANE VARNISH

Polyurethane protects surfaces and seals them from moisture. It is available in latex or oil-base formulas, tinted or clear, and in several sheens.

Stepladders are critical to have on hand for most wall paint projects. Consider investing in 3-foot and 6-foot ladders to help you safely and comfortably paint ceilings and walls of standard height. Know how your ladders lock open and avoid stepping on the top step while working. Many roller trays attach to ladders, and there are attachments to hold cans on ladders as well.

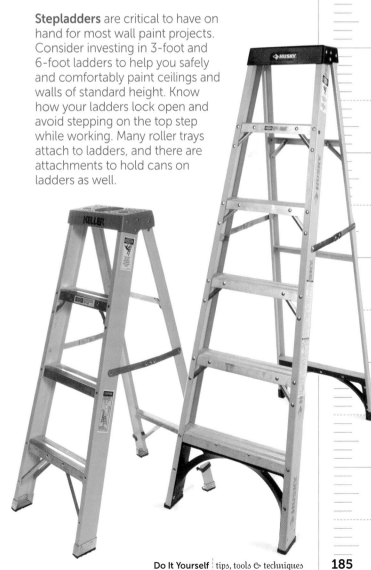

Prepping Your Room

Plan on devoting a full day to the four Ps: protecting the floors and fixtures, patching holes and gaps, prepping the surface, and priming the walls.

☐ Remove small items from the room and move large furniture into the center, covering it with a plastic or canvas drop cloth.

☐ Protect the floor with a drop cloth. Tape the edges to the floor to prevent slipping.

☐ Remove switchplates and outlet covers.

☐ Before painting woodwork, wash away dirt and residue with a TSP (trisodium phosphate) solution, then rinse trim several times with water and allow to dry thoroughly. Scrape away splintered or chipped wood, then sand with fine-grit (120- to 180-grit) paper. Wipe the woodwork with a tack cloth.

☐ Examine all surfaces for dents, holes, and cracks. Fill damaged wall surfaces with spackling paste and any woodwork with wood putty, smoothing dried ridges or lumps with 80-grit sandpaper. Caulk any gaps between trim and walls using paintable caulk, smoothing the caulking bead with a wet finger or damp sponge.

☐ Use painter's tape to tape off window and door frames, ceilings, baseboards, and other trim.

☐ Prime surfaces with the appropriate primer and allow to dry according to the manufacturer's directions. Now you're ready to paint!

paint finishes

Flat paint has a matte finish that's pretty much nonreflective, which is good for hiding wall blemishes. This finish does show scuffs and marks, so it's best in low-traffic areas—perfect for a ceiling.

Satin paint shows a slight luster with a soft texture. It's more durable than flat and works well in living rooms, dining rooms, and bedrooms.

Semigloss paint has a tougher skin than satin and a higher luster. It stands up well to cleaning and wear. It will show imperfections more readily than satin or flat paints. This finish works particularly well in kitchens and baths and on trim. It also is useful in narrow hallways where light is at a premium.

Gloss paint is hard, durable, and easy to clean, but its high luster makes imperfections clearly visible. Gloss is excellent for kitchen and bath cabinets.

Painting Your Room

step 1

LOAD YOUR BRUSH
Dip one-third of the brush's bristles into the paint. Lift the bristles out of the paint and gently tap them (don't wipe) against the rim of the paint can. The point is to load the brush with paint just short of dripping on the way to the wall.

step 2

CUT IN
Use a 3-inch flat brush to outline walls and ceilings—a technique known as "cutting in." An angled brush will work better in tricky areas that require more brush control. Leave a loosely brushed edge that allows the trimmed area to blend in when you paint the wall with a roller.

step 3

BRUSH IN SECTIONS
Apply the paint in long sections, each about two brush-widths wide. Brush upward to unload the brush, then down to set the paint, then up again to remove the brush marks.

TIP: Wrap the ferrule of the brush with painter's tape to catch drips.

step 4

USE A ROLLER
Load a roller by dipping it into a tray full of paint and rolling it up the tray's ramp until the roller is saturated. Work in small sections (4-foot areas), rolling paint onto the wall in an overlapping W motion. Be sure to overlap still-wet areas to prevent roller marks.

step 5

CLEAN BRUSHES
Remove excess paint with a wide-tooth comb. Rinse the brush in warm water or soak the brush in a solution of ½ cup liquid fabric softener to 1 gallon warm water for about 15 minutes. Attach your clean brush to a spin-drier tool by pushing the handle into the stiff spring clips, and spin inside a 5-gallon bucket to remove excess moisture.

step 6

STORE BRUSHES
Cut a rectangle of heavy kraft paper or grocery bag—twice the length of the ferrule and bristles and four times the width of the brush. Crease the paper vertically down the center. Place the brush on the paper edge and fold at the crease. Roll the brush into the paper. Secure it with a rubber band. Hang the brush by the handle or store it flat.

step 7

CLEAN ROLLERS
Scrape the excess paint out of the roller cover with the curved side of a five-in-one tool. Dump the paint back into the paint can. Rinse the cover in warm water, scraping with the tool until the water runs clean. Attach the cover to the spin-drier over the spring clips, and spin inside a 5-gallon bucket. Stand the roller cover on its end to dry completely before storing.

paint calculator

1. Calculate the wall area: Multiply the length of each wall by the height of the ceiling and add the products to arrive at your wall surface square footage.

2. If walls and doors account for more than 100 square feet in your room, deduct that amount from the wall area. Subtract 20 square feet for each door and 15 square feet for each window. Most rooms will not require this step.

3. Calculate the quantity of paint needed: Divide the total wall area by 400 square feet per gallon to get the quantity of paint needed per coat. For textured surfaces, divide by 300 square feet. Light colors usually need two coats, while dark colors may need three or more.

How to Paint Anything

Now that you're comfortable painting your walls, look around for other ways to employ your newfound confidence. A host of specialty paints and finishes can help you with any project. Using a variety of applications, you can paint your way to a whole new look.

BRICK

Scrub brick with a stiff brush, water, and mild detergent, then rinse with vinegar. For tough grime, use muriatic acid and rinse with 2 tablespoons baking soda per gallon of water. Apply masonry sealer and then use a long-nap foam roller to apply paint to the surface. Use a brush to get paint into the grout lines and crevices. If you have newly installed brick, wait 30 days before painting it.

CERAMICS & CERAMIC TILE

Wipe the surface clean and let dry. Use a paint formulated for ceramic or porcelain surfaces. Allow the paint to dry for several days or bake to cure according to the manufacturer's directions. If not using ceramic or porcelain paint, sand the surface lightly and clean with TSP (trisodium phosphate) cleaner to remove grease and dirt. When dry, apply a bonding or ceramic primer. Let the primer dry. Brush on latex paint in a gloss or semigloss finish.

FLOORCLOTH

Base-coat your rug material if desired. After the base coat dries, use a straightedge to guide your stencil placement. Apply your design in a contrasting color with a stencil brush and stencil, cleaning the stencil before moving it to a new section. When the paint is dry, seal and protect the design with clear polyurethane.

GLASS

Start with a clean, dry surface. If you use a pattern, tape it to the inside of clear glass. With an artist's brush, apply a thin layer of glass paint for a stained-glass look. For a more opaque finish, apply an additional coat after the first is dry. Paint slowly and gently to avoid bubbles. Using an artist's brush, seal the design with glass-paint varnish. If you want the look of frosted glass, use a varnish with a matte finish.

LAMINATE

Clean the surface with a cotton rag, water, and a mild detergent such as dish soap. Let dry, then sand with 180-grit or similar fine sandpaper. Wipe with a tack cloth. Apply a special bonding primer suitable for laminate surfaces to increase the paint's adhesion. Let dry according to the manufacturer's directions. Roll or spray a top coat paint that works with the primer applied. Consider testing products on a hidden area first.

CONCRETE

Scrub with TSP, then a bleach and water solution. Degrease oily spots using a concrete degreaser and repair cracks using concrete filler. Etch the surface with a 10 percent solution of muriatic acid and water. Apply a hydrodynamic sealer and two or three coats of paint specifically designed for concrete surfaces.

DRYWALL

Dust walls with a clean mop and wash them with TSP. Scrape off loose paint and fill any holes with surfacing compound. For new drywall, apply a wallboard sealer. For existing drywall, use a stain-blocking primer to help hide water stains. Apply two coats of latex paint, letting dry between coats.

FABRIC

Tape preshrunk fabric to plastic-treated cardboard. (Place the cardboard inside a pillow cover so paint doesn't soak through.) Use fabrics paint or an acrylic paint with textile medium added. Apply the paint in several thin coats to work it into the fibers. Heat set if required. Your piece can be laundered with mild detergent after 10–14 days.

METAL

Clean the surface with a stiff wire brush to remove flaking paint or rust. Wipe with a mixture of bleach and water using a damp cloth and let dry. Prime with metal primer and let dry, or use a paint specially formulated with rust inhibitors. Apply several thin coats of paint. If using spray paint, hold the can 10–12 inches from the surface as you spray. Shake the can during the application to keep the color mixed. Spray lightly to avoid paint runs.

PLASTIC

Sand the surface lightly to increase adhesion. Wash with TSP. Be careful not to touch the clean surface, leaving oil behind. Apply spray primer then spray paint, both designed for plastic. Apply multiple thin coats according to the manufacturer's directions and let dry between coats.

WOOD FURNITURE

If the surface is already painted or varnished, remove dirt or wax buildup with a household cleaner and rinse. Sand rough areas and wipe away dust with a tack cloth. Apply two coats of stain-blocking primer and allow it to dry between coats. Roll or brush on two coats of latex paint in the direction of the wood grain. Use a brush to finish the surface with smooth strokes.

project patterns

The following pages offer original design motifs you can reproduce for your paint projects. Refer to the project pages for complete instructions for how to use these designs as stencils, stamps, masks, screenprints, or transfers to aid in hand-painting. Patterns are not to size. Size as desired.

PAINT PROJECT PATTERNS FOR
Fabric & Textiles

PATTERNED PANELS
page 10

MAY I HAVE A WORD?
page 14

NATURE CALLS
page 17

CATCH OF THE DAY
page 20

COMING UP ROSES
page 18

TAKE A SEAT
page 25

LET'S FACE IT
page 28

SCREENPLAY
page 32

MR. ROBOTO
page 30

TABLE TOPPERS
page 34

PAINT PROJECT PATTERNS FOR
Furniture

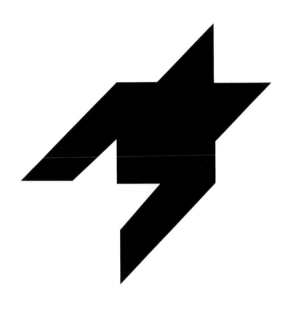

WAKE-UP CALL
page 38

DRESSER REDO
page 48

PETAL PUSHER
page 54

WICKER WONDERS
page 52

FRUIT PUNCH
page 51

Do It Yourself 100+ Paint Projects

BUDDING BEAUTY
page 56

Walls & Floors

WILLOWY WALLFLOWERS
page 72

PRETTY IN PINK
page 82

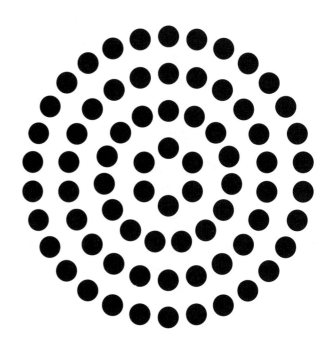

CLIMBING THE WALLS
page 77

DOT TO DOT
page 86

Do It Yourself 100+ Paint Projects

Artwork & Accessories

THIS CALLS FOR SECONDS
page 114

WALL FLOWERS
page 112

SHED SOME LIGHT
page 124

PRINTER'S BLOCK
page 126

PIXEL LOVE
page 133

PAINT PROJECT PATTERNS FOR
Ceramics, Glass & Metal

DISHING IT
page 144

PRECIOUS METALS
page 154

Cabinetry & Tile

AGED TO PERFECTION
page 164

AN APPLE A DAY
page 177

TILE TRANSFORMER
page 172

Sources

The sources for paints and paint tools are seemingly endless. Here are a few of the favorites we turned to for creating the projects in this book.

PRIMERS AND PAINTS

Behr
behr.com; 800/854-0133

Benjamin Moore
benjaminmoore.com;
800/672-4686

Dunn-Edwards Paints
dunnedwards.com;
888/337-2468

Dutch Boy
dutchboy.com;
800/828-5669

Farrow & Ball
farrow-ball.com;
888/511-1121

Glidden
glidden.com; 800/454-3336

Kilz
kilz.com; 800/325-3552

Martha Stewart Signature Color through Sherwin-Williams
sherwin-williams.com;
800/474-3794

Olympic
olympic.com; 800/441-9695

Pittsburgh Paints
ppgpittsburghpaints.com;
800/441-9695

Pratt & Lambert
prattandlambert.com;
800/289-7728

Sherwin-Williams
sherwin-williams.com;
800/474-3794

Valspar
valspar.com; 800/845-9061

ECO-FRIENDLY PAINTS

Anna Sova Healthy Paint—Anna Sova Luxury Organics
annasova.com; 214/742-7682

Benjamin Moore—Natura Zero-VOC
benjaminmoore.com;
800/672-4686

The Home Depot—The Freshaire Choice
homedepot.com;
800/466-3337

Mythic Paint
mythicpaint.com;
888/714-9422

The Old Fashioned Milk Paint Company
milkpaint.com;
978/448-6336

Olympic—Olympic Premium
olympic.com; 800/441-9695

Pittsburgh Paints—Pure Performance
ppgpittsburghpaints.com;
800/441-9695

Sherwin-Williams—Duration Home
sherwin-williams.com;
800/474-3794

Yolo Colorhouse
yolocolorhouse.com

CRAFTS PAINTS, SPRAY PAINTS, AND OTHER SPECIALTY PAINTS

A.C. Moore
acmoore.com;
888/226-6673

Belton Molotow
molotow.com

DecoArt
decoart.com;
800/367-3047

Delta Technical Coatings
deltacrafts.com;
800/423-4135

Hobby Lobby
hobbylobby.com

Hudson Paint
hudsonpaint.com;
845/758-3229

Krylon Products Group
krylon.com; 800/832-2541

Michaels
michaels.com

Plaid Enterprises, Inc.
(Folkart and Apple Barrel brand crafts paints)
plaidonline.com;
800/842-4197

Rust-Oleum Corp.
rust-oleum.com;
800/747-9767

Sharpie
sharpie.com; 800/346-3278

HOME IMPROVEMENT STORES

Ace Hardware
acehardware.com;
866/290-5334

The Home Depot
homedepot.com;
800/466-3337

Lowes
lowes.com; 800/445-6937

Walmart
walmart.com; 800/925-6278

STENCILS

Cutting Edge Stencils
cuttingedgestencils.com;
201/828-9146

Designer Stencils
designerstencils.com;
800/822-7836

Dressler Stencil Company
dresslerstencils.com;
888/656-4515

Royal Design Studio
royaldesignstudio.com;
800/747-9767

Stencil Ease
stencilease.com;
800/334-1776

Stencil Library
stencil-library.com

Wall to Wall Stencils
walltowallstencils.com;
317/598-0029

PAINTER'S TAPE

3M Scotch Blue
scotchblue.com

Frogtape
frogtape.com;
877/376-4827

Shurtape
shurtape.com;
888/442-8273

PAINTBRUSHES, ROLLERS, AND TRAYS

Purdy Corporation
purdycorp.com;
800/547-0780

Shur-Line
shurline.com; 877/748-7546

Wooster Brush Company
woosterbrush.com;
800/392-7246

Whizz
whizzrollers.com;
800/767-7038

PAINT LADDERS AND STEPLADDERS

Rubbermaid
rubbermaid.com;
888/895-2110

Werner
wernerladder.com;
888/523-3370

Xtend & Climb
xtendandclimb.com;
612/330-9915

PAINT SPRAYERS

Graco
graco.com; 800/690-2894

Wagner
wagnerspraytech.com;
800/328-8251

Project Index